Lean Daily Management for Healthcare

A Strategic Guide to Implementing Lean for Hospital Leaders

Sessions:

{ 7 July 1st

22 25,4179

Consensus

Lean Daily Management for Healthcare

A Strategic Guide to Implementing Lean for Hospital Leaders

Brad White

CRC Press
Taylor & Francis Group
Boca Raton   London   New York

CRC Press is an imprint of the
Taylor & Francis Group, an **informa** business

A PRODUCTIVITY PRESS BOOK

CRC Press
Taylor & Francis Group
6000 Broken Sound Parkway NW, Suite 300
Boca Raton, FL 33487-2742

© 2016 by Brad White
CRC Press is an imprint of Taylor & Francis Group, an Informa business

No claim to original U.S. Government works

Printed on acid-free paper
Version Date: 20160414

International Standard Book Number-13: 978-1-4987-5898-7 (Paperback)

Library of Congress Cataloging-in-Publication Data

Names: White, Brad (Bradley Steven), 1980- , author.
Title: Lean daily management for healthcare : a strategic guide to implementing lean for hospital leaders / Brad White.
Description: Boca Raton, FL : CRC Press, 2016.
Identifiers: LCCN 2015050131 | ISBN 9781498758987 (pbk.)
Subjects: | MESH: Health Facility Administration--methods | Health Services Administration | Efficiency, Organizational | Total Quality Management
Classification: LCC RA971 | NLM WX 155 | DDC 362.1068--dc23
LC record available at http://lccn.loc.gov/2015050131

**Visit the Taylor & Francis Web site at
http://www.taylorandfrancis.com**

**and the CRC Press Web site at
http://www.crcpress.com**

Printed and bound in the United States of America by Sheridan

To nurses everywhere. The future of healthcare is, and always has been, in your hands. As such, the future is bright.

Contents

Preface

Building a thriving Lean program that delivers results, improves the culture, and sustains its gains is no easy feat. There are a plethora of consultants selling tools and workshops that promise much, yet deliver little. Lean tools are paraded as the answer, yet each is taught as a stand-alone solution rather than an integrated approach to fundamentally improving how care is delivered.

The goal of this book is to cut through the clutter and noise that have been generated by Lean, Six Sigma, and other process improvement gurus. You do not need more tools, more programs, or more workshops to improve your hospital. What you need is a simple, consistent approach to manage problem-solving.

This approach is *Lean Daily Management*. With consistent rounding, a few whiteboards, pen-and-paper data, and a focused effort on working the plan–do–study–act cycle, you can build a common problem-solving bench strength throughout your organization. Once this is done, your people will be ready to use the more complex tools, workshops, and *kaizen* events because the larger framework on which all future improvements can be hung will have been built.

It is a management system that breaks down barriers among the frontline staff, directors, and the administrator team and empowers the frontline staff to take the lead on problem-solving by providing the training and tools with which they can identify and solve their own problems.

The mechanics of Lean Daily Management focus on the problem-solving boards. Here, metrics are tracked, data are gathered, root-cause analysis is performed, and reports are given on daily morning rounds. These morning rounds enable the administrative team to engage in problem-solving with frontline staff in their individual departments and then return to the administration board to recap a realistic vision of the current status of the hospital.

This book is intended to act as a guide, a road map, of how to roll out a Lean Daily Management system from start to finish. The book is split into three parts: (1) preparation, (2) implementation, and (3) production, each covering in greater detail how to apply what you have learned. For those who are brave enough to try building this on their own, this book will give you a complete overview of what the finished product should look like and how to get there. For those who choose to bring in outside help, either a consultant or a full-time Lean coach, this book will help you speak the same language and understand where that person is taking the organization. Where he or she departs from this approach will become evident, and he or she will be able to explain why a departure is necessary, as it so often is.

Section I, Preparation, covers the philosophy and thinking behind Lean Daily Management. This part is critical because so much of the implementation of the system will require your leadership to think about their role in the organization differently.

Section II, Implementation, is a nuts-and-bolts guide to building your own program. It covers everything from how to set up a rounding schedule to how to physically assemble the boards. It breaks down the cultural change into distinct, measurable phases with detailed instructions for leadership at all levels of the organization at each phase.

Section III, Production, looks at specific applications for your new management system. Pulling on the experience of dozens of hospitals from throughout the United States, sample approaches are shared on how to improve discharge times, patient satisfaction, clinical quality, and more.

In addition to the material in this book, all the templates for the boards, training material, and instructional packets are available for free download at LeanDailyManagement.com in an easy-to-edit format. My hope is that you take it, use it, improve it, and share it with others.

Prepare for the change to be disruptive. Lean Daily Management is not complementary to your current Lean efforts. It will not mesh seamlessly with your current use of kaizens, A3s, value stream mapping efforts, or project management. The reason is that Lean Daily Management is not the missing piece that will round out your Lean program. Instead, it is the missing foundation that will revolutionize your Lean program. Lean Daily Management is the start of the Lean journey, not the end.

Administrators should have no illusions about the discipline and commitment that will be required of them. Lean Daily Management is not a management tool; it is a management system, and, as such, there is a steep learning curve for leaders as they rethink their role in the organization. Administrators must become students, coaches, teachers, and scientific problem-solvers all at once. Learning any one of these roles can be challenging—learning all four at once is incredibly frustrating. Effective leaders must find a way to relinquish old habits and methods of managing while learning new techniques. Embracing Lean Daily Management will produce better staff and better administrators but not without effort on the part of everyone who is involved.

Consequently, the rewards for mastering Lean Daily Management are significant. Employee engagement issues will become a thing of the past; future process improvement projects will start with the benefit of a proven process that involves frontline leaders and problem-solvers, and seemingly intractable problems will become attainable opportunities as the hospital's problem-solving abilities increase. Finally, by building a daily habit of working through problems with the appropriate tools for structure and discipline, the hospital will become a true learning organization.

Developing Lean hospitals is more than helping them survive the coming changes in healthcare or even thrive financially. For me, Lean hospitals represent a more humane way to deliver care—for patients and their families, staff, physicians, and, yes, even administrators. I am passionate about the potential improved operations management for the future of healthcare in the United States, and I believe that the people best situated to fixing healthcare in this country are you and your staff. I wish you all the best as you begin your Lean journey!

Brad White

Acknowledgments

Writing a book seems such a simple task. You just sit down and write, preferably with coffee and, if life is exceptionally kind, a large dog. Reality, though, is a bit different. Years of stumbling, screwing up, and starting over are step 1. At some point, hopefully, some sort of success starts to materialize. This book is an effort to codify that success and project what future success might look like. This path requires great patience, mostly not from the one walking it. In no particular order, I thank the following people.

First, I thank Dr. Frank Chen and the entire engineering department at the University of Texas at San Antonio. Not only do they provide world-class engineering training, but also they were willing to take a gamble on a business major and set me on the Lean path.

Jerry Berlanga has been a faithful *sensei*, ever-enduring in the face of my confrontational learning style. Without his self-less, continuous investment in my development, I would be years from where I am now.

Greg Uhlig has been both a close friend and a mentor. He is a constant source for sage advice that I turn to when confronted with a challenge.

Heather Anderson, Sam Spencer, and the team at Baptist Health System in San Antonio deserve a huge shout-out (and sanity check) for being the first hospital system that was willing to hire me. I learned a tremendous amount under their tutelage. When many would have held me back, they pushed me forward.

I am forever grateful to Trey Lisbayne and Alex Maldonado for elevating my career to the national stage. I learned more in my short time with them about systematizing Lean than at any other time.

Much of my understanding of Lean Daily Management came from two of my mentees, Hurley Smith and Jaime Alonzo. They pushed their Lean understanding beyond my own and taught me much in the process.

This book would not be possible without the huge vote of confidence that Rod Huebbers gave me when he brought me into University Health in Shreveport, Louisiana. Not only did I get to run my own system and try my ideas, I also met two people who, despite their better judgments, decided to take me under their wings and carry me to success. Rebecca Wozniak and Shirley Repta, thank you so much, and I love you both!

Huge thanks go to my brother, Jacob White, and mother, Janet White, for their incredible support while I was writing this book. My sister-in-law, Ashley White, also deserves a shout-out for her incredible hospitality in always making me feel welcome.

I owe my father, G. Steven White, both great thanks and a twinge of blame for his incessant, relentless focus on the patients, and only the patients, to the chagrin of administration and the powers that be.

My entire San Antonio crew—Elicia White, Caitlin Barclay, Courtney Hobson, Alyssa Petko, Jon and Alex Fischer, and Lauren and Miguel Ayala—has been such a constant through not only this book but also my entire career and it is high time I finally said "thank you." I am blessed with friends whom I do not deserve.

The simple encouragement of David Goldberg during the writing process cannot be ignored. Not only was David successful in implementing Lean Daily Management, he also continually reached out and encouraged me when the idea of a book seemed a far and ethereal dream.

This last bit is equal parts respect and thanks, and it is by no means last in order of importance. To the members of the 525 MI BDE, I count it a great honor that, for a few brief moments, I was fortunate enough to count myself among you. There are too many to thank individually, and all of them are like brothers and sisters to me, but a couple of names stand tall among the giants. First, I owe much to Amy Torguson. There is nothing that can compare to the confidence of one soldier in another. Second, undying respect to Amanda Older. You are why I do what I do. I will miss you always.

Finally, to the large dog, Moko, thanks for the many hours of companionship and warm feet! May we have many more years together.

Brad White

Author

Brad White is a Lean Six Sigma Master Black Belt and earned an MS in advanced manufacturing and enterprise engineering from the University of Texas at San Antonio. He helped build the Lean Daily Management program for the Baptist Health System in San Antonio, Texas, expanded that program at Tenet Health, and led the team who implemented the program at University Health in northern Louisiana. He continues to write about, develop, and share Lean thinking at LeanDailyManagement.com. He can be reached at Brad@LeanDailyManagement.com.

Introduction

Our prevailing system of management has destroyed our people.

Dr. Deming

It is no secret that hospital management is becoming an increasingly challenging proposition. Declining reimbursement and the growing complexity of care have put a significant squeeze on operating margins. This trend is likely to continue as the United States spends nearly 50% more as a percentage of gross domestic product than the next highest industrialized nation, almost double the Organisation for Economic Co-operation and Development average, with equal or slightly poorer returns to show for it.* From the perspective of policy makers, healthcare costs should decline by a third to half in order to be brought into line with the rest of the industrialized world, and they have serious motivation to do so.

Healthcare spending accounted for 27% of the federal budget in 2015. More money was spent on healthcare than on defense and education put together.† On average, states spend 16% of their budget on healthcare (although that ranges

---

* The United States spent 17.6% of gross domestic product on healthcare in 2012. The next highest spender was the Netherlands at 12% (http://www.pbs.org/newshour /rundown/health-costs-how-the-us-compares-with-other-countries/).
† Available at http://www.usgovernmentspending.com/federal_budget_detail _fy12os12015n_10#usgs302.

significantly from state to state).* These numbers should come as no surprise to industry insiders. Much political hay has been made of soaring healthcare costs, and much more will be made until those costs are contained.

It is very tempting as hospital operators to blame the myriad problems that exist outside of our control. Prescription drug costs are much higher in the United States than elsewhere. Insurance companies and HMOs take too large a cut. Physicians operate independently and not in the best interests of the overall system. Excessive governmental regulation cripples efficient operations. The list goes on. These observations are as useless as they are correct in the sense that they are beyond our control as hospital managers.

The problem is this: hospital costs account for 32% of total healthcare spending—the largest segment of our healthcare dollar.† Physicians and clinics, the next largest segment, claim only 20% of total spending. Prescription drug costs are under 10%. From the perspective of policy makers, the message is clear: in order to reduce healthcare spending, we must pay hospitals less, much less.

While this, at first glance, seems to be an incredibly bleak prognosis, there are a couple of major opportunities that hospital administrators can leverage: (a) people and (b) process.

Hospital employees are among the most highly trained work force of any industry. The bulk of them have a bachelor's degree or better. Many of those who do not are on degree-seeking paths. It is not uncommon to find frontline staff with PhDs. In terms of raw intellect, the average hospital sits atop a gold mine.

Not only are hospital staff highly trained, but they also are arguably the most compassionate and most highly motivated of any work force. Very few nurses enter the field solely for

---

* Available at http://www.cbpp.org/research/policy-basics-where-do-our-state-tax-dollars-go.
† Available at http://www.cms.gov/Research-Statistics-Data-and-Systems/Statistics-Trends-and-Reports/NationalHealthExpendData/downloads/highlights.pdf.

financial security. They are natural caregivers and thrive on delivering excellent patient care. Shrewd hospital management can leverage these two aspects of the work force to deliver high-quality, low-cost care consistently.

The second major opportunity that hospitals have is their own management style. Systems thinking has yet to penetrate most hospital executive teams to the degree that it has in other industries. This systems thinking allows the hospital to move beyond the fog and chaos that plague day-to-day operations by providing a platform for continuous, consistent, and sustainable improvements that happen throughout the entire organization every day.

The majority of efforts to improve processes in hospitals has been through the deployment of Lean or Six Sigma teams or experts and engineers. There has been a heavy emphasis on training, certification, and project work, yet results have remained elusive. Scores of people are trained, yet it results in little tangible improvement. Engineers, Black Belts, and consultants tackle large obstacles with great initial success, yet, within a few months, the problems reappear. The process improvement team is stuck in an eternal battle to prove the impact that they have had on the bottom line. Staff engagement is low, and leadership is ready to move on to the next thing.

The problem is not that focusing on process improvement is wrong or that the Lean- and Six Sigma–type approaches do not work. They can, but they need the right environment in which they can be successful. More training will not change the culture. More projects and experts will not change the culture. The only thing that can change the culture is a new way of managing both process improvement and the daily operations of the hospital. What this means is that the Lean team can no longer be a fire-and-forget weapon that is deployed by leadership to fix things. Instead, leadership must roll up their sleeves and engage daily in improvement if the improvement is going to truly be successful. What is needed is a new system of management.

The goal of this book is to provide a road map for deploying a management system that engages your work force and aligns them with the strategic direction of the hospital so that, every day, quality improves, costs decrease, and your people become an ever-more-valuable asset.

The Current State of Management

In order to understand our current approach to management, it is necessary to understand how we developed it. As it turns out, the rise of the automobile had a profound and lasting impact on how American businesses manage themselves.*

In the early 1900s, Henry Ford first cracked the code on how to mass-produce automobiles cheaply for the masses. His secret was simple—eliminate any and all variation. He once famously said that customers could have any color of car that they wanted "so long as it was black." The rigorous standard-ization was so tight that the physical structure of the factory in Dearborn, Michigan was designed around specific components flowing down to the assembly area.

This strategy was highly successful so long as there was no need for product variety. In the 1920s, General Motors (GM) exploited this weakness by building a conglomerate of auto-motive manufacturers. What they lost in production cost, they made up for in marketing and distribution efficiencies. GM quickly became the dominant auto maker, and their growth strategy was simple—if a company could be bought and deliver a high-enough return on investment (ROI), GM would make the purchase. If not, they would move on.

By the 1950s, GM was such a powerhouse that this ROI decision model became entrenched in the then-developing business curriculum at universities everywhere. While GM would maintain its dominance for another two decades, a small loom company in Japan decided to enter the automobile

---

* *Toyota Kata* (2009) by Mike Rother provides a much more exhaustive description of the rise of the American management system.

market. Toyota, with no automobile experience and few natural resources, started down a path of continuous improvement that would ultimately culminate in them dethroning GM for the title of the largest automotive manufacturer in the world.

While GM continued to acquire businesses, Toyota became obsessive about chasing waste out of their own processes. They pioneered ideas such as flexible manufacturing (the ability to produce several vehicles simultaneously on one line) and one-piece flow (which allowed them to drastically reduce inventory levels). When the 1970's gas crisis hit, GM was caught flat footed. Toyota had long dominated the market for small fuel-efficient vehicles. Suddenly, GM found itself fighting on Toyota's turf and saddled by excessive investments in vehicles that the market no longer wanted.

GM's woes were only beginning though. Because they had bought instead of built their way to market dominance, they were unable to keep up with the pace of improvements at Toyota. Not only was Toyota getting better, but it was also doing so at a faster pace than GM could match.

GM was facing a situation that is similar to what hospitals are facing now. The market for cars had largely been saturated, meaning further growth through acquisition was no longer viable, and there was a much greater focus on the cost and quality of the product than there had ever been before. Interestingly, because GM wrote a book on American management, hospitals are currently responding with the same failed approach that GM did. Fortunately, there is another way.

Continuous Improvement versus ROI Thinking

GM's approach to management in a growing market made a lot of sense. It allowed them to rapidly expand and engulf potential competitors. A relentless focus on financial metrics led to smart acquisitions that quickly dropped profit to the bottom line. Problems did not arise until there were no longer profitable companies to buy, and the current portfolio began to turn sour.

Using the same financial thinking that grew the company, GM turned its focus to cutting costs. The only problem is that GM did not know how to eliminate waste, so it decided to simply spend less instead. After all, according to the ROI formula, when returns (profits) drop, investments (expenses) should drop proportionally to maintain equilibrium. Layoffs ensued; quality dropped; and sales slacked. Like so many businesses that followed its management style, GM was caught with an operation that it did not really know how to control.

Toyota also used ROI thinking but did so differently. Toyota utilized it as an operational tool, not a financial decision maker. When confronted with a necessary investment in the business, Toyota looked at the ROI. If the return justified the expenditure, like GM, they proceeded. Unlike GM, if the investment did not make financial sense, they worked on the operational details until it did. What waste could be removed? What extra value could be built in? The question was not whether or not to invest but rather what must be done before the investment was sound.

This continuous effort toward improvement bequeathed Toyota with two major advantages when the gas crisis hit. First, their assembly lines were inherently more efficient. Second, their people knew how to make operational improvements that dropped to the bottom line instead of relying on budget cuts and layoffs.*

---

* Toyota has only had one layoff as part of it closing down their operations in Australia. By relying on cross-training, temp-to-hire, and a long-term view on the value of human capital, the company has weathered ups and downs without sacrificing its work force.

The Coming Changes in How We Manage Hospitals

This transcends industry. Like GM, healthcare finds itself at the outer limits of what acquisition and growth are able to deliver. There is a finite amount of new businesses and new markets that can be tapped to deliver ever-increasing ROIs. As the industry approaches maturity, it is becoming increasingly difficult to grow into more profitability. Growth is finally beginning to approach the rate of overall economic growth, meaning that, in order to grow any faster, one health system must sacrifice for another because it is becoming a zero-sum game.

This is not all bad; it is merely a change. It is a shifting of the gears from aggressive acceleration to high-speed cruising. The crux of success is no longer how to acquire new businesses; rather, it is how to deliver the current business better, faster, and cheaper. Fortunately, hospitals do not need to blaze a trail through virgin territory. Toyota provides an excellent case study on how to not only survive the coming transition but also be poised to take a dominant role in the new healthcare economy.

The secret to Toyota's success lies in its systematic approach to its people. Much has been written about its Lean approach to manufacturing and the tools that it uses to achieve those results, but, without the underlying management system and employee culture to support those tools, they are all for naught. Like the finest of carpentry tools in the hands of novices, these tools cannot improve a business until the business first improves its people.

This paints the way forward for American hospitals. By implementing a management system that leverages and unleashes the skills of their people, hospitals stand more than a fighting chance to survive—they have the opportunity to redefine how healthcare is delivered to their community. American hospitals are faced with the task of drastically reducing the cost of healthcare. Fortunately, they are well equipped to do so.

PREPARATION

Well begun is half done.

Aristotle

There is a strong tendency among healthcare leaders to jump straight from problem recognition to solution. So much of a Lean Daily Management system depends on leaders resisting this urge. Just as the first step to solving a problem is truly understanding it, the first step to implementing a Lean management system is to understand the thinking behind one.

The best-formed implementation plan is only as good as the individuals implementing it, because the plan itself only survives through the opening phases of implementation. As Helmuth von Moltke observed, no plan survives contact with the enemy. Inevitably, things change. Resistances shift. The inherent complexity of hospital operations ensures that time-tables will shift and accommodations must be made.

The goal of this section is to prepare you to be able to handle these unforeseen complications. You will find through this process that what is done is not nearly so important as why it is done. If you can understand the why behind a decision, then you can weather the times when the wrong thing is done for the right reasons.

Given the challenges facing the industry—declining reimbursement and increasing complexity of care—a new system of managing is needed. The key, it turns out, is to return to a true definition of quality.

Chapter 1

Impact of Quality

Quality is not an act. It is a habit.

Aristotle

Introduction

Quality is often used as an ambiguous term, an interchangeable synonym with *good*. We talk about a quality car, or quality construction, or even our patients receiving quality care. In each of these cases, the word is used as a handle to convey a much larger concept, one that the rest of this book will center around. That larger concept can be thought of loosely as the product or service doing what it was supposed to do.

For instance, if a car breaks down shortly after being driven off the lot, that is not a quality car. If it breaks down after 250,000 miles, then it was most assuredly a quality car. Likewise, if a house does not last 10 years, the construction was not quality construction. If it needs work done after 50 years, then it was. What, then, is quality healthcare?

What Is Quality?

Quality is fairly easily defined as *meeting or exceeding customer requirements*. That intuitively makes sense when applied to cars and houses, but it becomes much more complex and less satisfying when applied to healthcare. The reason is twofold.

First, healthcare is much more complex than cars and houses. For instance, regardless of make or model, all consumer cars should last at least 10 years or 100,000 miles. Regardless of the type or size of house, the location built, or the materials used, the construction should generally last at least 50 years. Anything less is defective. In the hospital though, it is much fuzzier. Patients are there for a wide range of ailments, representing every stage of life, with a diverse range of acuities. What metric can be applied universally to gauge the quality of the care that is delivered to them?

Efforts have been made to do this. Core measures are an attempt to objectively judge quality. They do not take into account though the patients who do not fall under the measures or care that is provided outside of the measures. This has led to hospitals becoming more focused on the measure than the care for very understandable reasons. Patient satisfaction is another approach to the problem, with the underlying assumption being that if the patients are happy, they must have received quality care. The problems with this approach are that the patients do not understand what is best clinically and satisfaction is not a direct measurement of clinical quality. This has led to hospitals pouring effort and money into nonclinical activities such as free valet parking and stunningly beautiful campuses. In extreme cases, it leads to a compromise of safety for satisfaction, such as allowing patients to refuse surgical site markings for cosmetic reasons.

Second, the generic definition of meeting or exceeding customer requirements falls flat in the hospital is that, as healthcare professionals, it is very difficult to see our business

from the perspective of the patients. While their perception of an outpatient surgery is the parking area, the main
entrance of the hospital, the registration process, pre-op, and
recovery, we see all of the invisible components that must
work behind the scenes to pull off the procedure. We see the
supplies, logistics, wrangling with physician groups, negoti-
ating with the vendors, room turns, environmental services,
insurance verifications, and so on. It becomes very difficult
to simplify our vision to that of the customer. How can we
possibly satisfy a range of customer satisfaction requirements
while balancing the myriad trade-offs that occur behind the
scenes?

The problem then is this: a generic definition of quality
does not work in the hospital because the system is too complex and the perspective of the patient is too far removed from
the actual work that must take place. Because the solution to a
problem lies in grasping a true understanding of the problem,
let us dig into each of these.

Hospital Complexity

Hospital complexity is driven by a number of things.
Regulation, the range of services offered, physician preference, patients, and a host of other factors combine to greatly
complicate operations. Very little of this lies within the control of the hospital administration. Regulations cannot be
ignored or easily altered, and patients cannot be turned away.
Thus, those two sources of complexity will always remain.
Physicians can be influenced to some degree, and the range
of services offered can be pared down.* Neither of these are
easy to accomplish, and most hospitals have no interest in
reducing their volume for very good reasons. So, it seems,

---

* An excellent example of this is the stand-alone clinics that take nonemergency
  patients. By focusing on one thing only, they can streamline their business
  to become incredibly profitable while undercutting the hospital emergency
  department on pricing.

there is little that can be done to reduce the complexity of hospital operations at this point. (Once a daily management system is up and running, operations can be simplified as shown later in this book. At this stage though, the focus needs to be on managing the current system rather than simplifying it.)

If complexity cannot be reduced at the moment, then it must be better managed and controlled. There is no other alternative. As more and more treatment options become available, hospital operations will continue to grow in complexity. In their book *Waging War on Complexity Costs*, Stephen Wilson and Andrei Perumal point out that "complexity is the single greatest determinant of your cost-competitiveness."* This helps clarify the challenge facing hospital administrations everywhere. The work required to manage the hospital continues to increase, whereas the leadership bandwidth to do so remains stagnant. If this is the true root of the problem, then the solution is to find a way to increase the bandwidth of leadership without increasing the cost of overhead. While this sounds impossible, it can be done by using the military concept of a *force multiplier*. By handing over daily management to the frontline staff, hospital leaders can remove themselves from the management role and instead become true leaders. The bulk of this book covers in exacting detail how to do this.

Patient Perspective Lost

The second core problem is that the perspective of the patient, or the *voice of the customer*, is lost. There is little linkage between the daily activities of frontline staff and the ultimate delivery of value to the patient, meaning that there is not a

---

* *Waging War on Complexity Costs: Reshape Your Cost Structure, Free Up Cash Flows and Boost Productivity by Attacking Process, Product and Organizational Complexity*, Wilson, Stephen and Perumal, Andrei, McGraw-Hill, 2009, xiii. This book excellently delves into tackling the complexity in any organization, how to separate the good complexity from the bad, and how to eliminate it.

clear understanding of how those daily activities impact the final care that patients receive. This linkage is difficult to achieve due to the complexity of hospital operations, but it can be done.

The way to accomplish this is to first define who the internal and external customers are for the core processes and then to break down the customer requirements into operational metrics that a process must continually achieve to deliver defect-free results. In essence, what is needed is systems engineering.

A common objection to this is that hospital systems are too complex to undergo such engineering. In reality, the more complex a system is, the more engineering it needs. A simple footbridge can be built with little or no engineering done. The Golden Gate Bridge though is an engineering marvel because of the complexity of the physics that was solved through rigorous design.

In a similar fashion, hospital systems need to be designed precisely because it is so difficult to do so. The design needed goes far beyond policies and procedures or even detailed process mapping. What is lacking is a granular understanding of how to break down quality into metrics that must be hit. Often, they are broken down as a percentage (such as percent overtime) or an average (such as average discharge times). While this seems logical, in practice, this rarely works as well as planned.

A good example of what is needed can be seen in producing a car. New vehicles are advertised as having a 10-year or 100,000-mile warranty. This can be thought of as the voice of the customer. When the customer buys this vehicle, he or she sets a very clear, established expectation before the transaction is made. This becomes the overarching definition of quality for that vehicle.

Now, imagine that you are running that car factory. How do you achieve that result? Do you constantly remind people that quality is everything? Do you establish clear punishments for employees who build cars that do not outlast the warranty? Do you pull everyone off the line once a year and have them hear stories about families who are stranded when their vehicles prematurely broke? Of course not. Yet, hospitals regularly employ similar approaches to deliver quality. The problem is that using only the final determinant of quality is an impossible way to manage operations on a daily basis to deliver the said quality. What must be done is that the ultimate quality goal must be broken down for each area that contributes to it.

So, if a vehicle must last 100,000 miles, then the engine must be able to turn at least 200 million revolutions. We can now test each engine component to see if they can reliably last 200 million revolutions. This, in turn, will dictate the manufacturing tolerances for specific components. For instance, the gap between the piston and the cylinder must be within a certain range; otherwise, wear and tear will happen faster than is acceptable. Breaking this down further, the specific dimensions of the piston itself can be developed. Any piece that is within that range is considered a quality piece; any piece that is outside is considered a defect.

If the previous paragraph confused you, that is the point. If other industries can break down the definition of a quality product into a product with myriad specific, well-defined qualities, then hospitals can as well. Before tackling the question of how to do so, consider the benefits.

Poor quality can be stopped before it ever impacts the customer. By continuously measuring all of the components, catching and correcting defects as they happen, and then correcting the defective process that created them, not only is quality assured on the back end, but also the effort to deliver that quality becomes increasingly cheaper. Also, as the plant manager, you do not have to know everything about the creation of the vehicle because you have a quality management system that tells you, in black and white, how you are doing in real time. Your job is not to determine what quality is anymore—that is the role of the subject-matter experts. Your job now is to ensure that those metrics are hit and, when they are not, that the organization corrects the problem and improves itself. As Aristotle said, "Quality is a habit." It must become the habit of the entire organization, including management. This is difficult because good habits require discipline. Your role is to provide that discipline.

There are two questions regarding quality that every leader, regardless of level, must answer:

1. Do you care about quality?
2. What are you going to do about it?

Sadly, the answer to the first question is not always a genuine yes. If it is not for you, then there is nothing that this book can, or should, help you with. However, if you and your organization are committed to quality, then the rest of this book will help you answer the second question.

This book will provide a map of the terrain that your hospital must cross if it is to thrive in the coming environment. Like any map, this book is an oversimplification of what must be done. The journey is always harder than the planning, and this will be no exception. There will be times when the enthusiasm for the journey will be near euphoric. Then, there will come times when the temptation and cries to quit will seem insurmountable. You and your fellow leaders will go through a painful process of learning to let go of the illusion of control. Your managers must learn to become vulnerable in front of both their people and their bosses. Your employees will need to find the courage to speak out and reveal their own mistakes.

Through all of this, there is one, and only one, determinant of success. Regardless of the capability of the management, the morale of the staff, the presence or absence of a union, the financial constraints of the hospital, or the cooperation of the physicians, the only thing that dictates success or failure is the quality and consistency of the senior leadership. If your organization starts this journey and fails, it is because senior leadership abandoned the path. If the transformation is a resounding success, it will be because leadership weathered the storms that will inevitably come. Of course, by the time the change is successful, leadership will be muted and in the background as frontline staff owns the win.

This journey is not a short one. Be prepared to work at this for three to five years before large successes are realized. You will have small wins almost instantaneously, followed by a long stretch of invisible progress. People will want to abandon the program, saying that it does not work anymore. Stick with it anyway. As problems are unveiled, people will become threatened. At some point, a physician will speak out against what you are doing. Stick with it anyway. Some of your managers will be so threatened by the program that they will walk away. Stick with it anyway. If your leadership team refuses to quit, the end result will be a hospital that enjoys an engaged work force, systematically develops future leaders, continuously improves patient care and physician satisfaction, and uncovers and eliminates waste on a daily basis.

Chapter 2

The Role of Leadership

To become a leader, you must first become a human being.

Confucius

Introduction

Underestimating the size of the cultural change needed is one of the most common mistakes that leadership makes when implementing a Lean program. All too often, leaders and process improvement practitioners place too much focus on Lean tools and methodologies and do not focus enough on the people and human structure of the organization. Lean Daily Management often enjoys dramatic, albeit a touch flashy, success early in its adoption simply because it corrects this imbalance. The challenge for leaders is to learn how to fundamentally shift their own core beliefs and values so that they can shift the culture of the people who are under them.

Early on, in the deployment of Lean Daily Management, most leaders feel exceedingly vulnerable as they begin to let go of the reigns and let frontline staff start making decisions. This is a complete turn from how most hospital leaders operate. Command and control is a much more common leadership style because it feels more secure. The grim reality though is that rarely can you have both command *and* control—there is a natural trade-off between the two that becomes more pronounced the more complex the work is.

The reasoning is simple. In an environment where work is visible, defects are easily spotted, and variation is minimal, there is little use for complex problem-solving. A small handful of managers can identify and correct issues as they arise. Henry Ford, who simplified work by producing one type of one car, reportedly lamented, *"Why is it every time I ask for a pair of hands, they come with a brain attached?"* Command and control works in that environment. Unfortunately, healthcare is nothing like a simplistic assembly line.

In the hospital, work is hidden, defects are difficult to detect, and variation is among the highest of any industry. The work is hidden because it is not readily apparent what the status of the current work is. For instance, if we were to visit a well-run manufacturing floor, we would instantly know where problems were occurring simply by looking at where the line stopped moving. However, if we were to walk out onto a nursing floor during medication pass, it would be difficult to tell which patients had received medication and which had not. Similarly, it would be difficult to know where the floor is in the discharge planning process. Both of these processes could be at a dead stop, yet that would be obscured by the constant movement that is common to a nursing floor.

On the manufacturing floor, defects would be easy to spot. Pieces would not fit together; quality check points would pile up with bad parts, creating a visual cue for managers; and simple alerts would sound when a machine or operator detected an error. Return to the nursing floor though, and we are unable to see errors. Mixed-up medication is difficult to detect. Defects in our fall prevention measures require laborious inspection to check. While on the manufacturing floor, we can see and manage defects, on the hospital floor, we can only see the staff, so we attempt to manage them instead. This leads naturally to a very punitive culture where people are held accountable for their mistakes. While this makes leaders feel good, it ultimately buries quality issues, allowing them to fester undetected like a slow infection until they burst forth in crisis.

Punitively holding people accountable for mistakes creates a culture that values hiding problems over fixing problems simply because when problems are exposed, people are punished. Aubrey Daniels, in his book *Bringing Out the Best in People* (1999),* points out that it is not the *antecedents* (telling people what to do) that create behavior but rather the *consequences* (what happens to them after the behavior occurs). Thus, you can tell people to be careful all you would like, and to speak up when something goes wrong, but punishing a mistake is not only punishing the mistake—it is also punishing the revelation of the mistake. From the perspective of the employee, the negative consequence of making a mistake can be thwarted simply by hiding it. This makes defects, already difficult to spot, near invisible.

Shifting to a *red-is-good* mentality can help overcome this reluctance to share. By thanking and rewarding staff for revealing mistakes and creating a safe environment for sharing, leaders can encourage self-reporting of errors.

The last major observation we may make on the manufacturing floor is how regular and cadenced everything is. With job cycles timed down to the second, one of the largest health threats to manufacturing workers is repetitive motion injuries. The product only varies slightly, so the work requires only minor adjustments to keep pace. The nursing floor is the polar opposite. Patients of different sizes, with differences in diagnoses, acuities, disposition, locations, physicians, social and

---

* *Bringing Out the Best in People: How to Apply the Astonishing Power of Positive Reinforcement* is a must-read for anyone in a leadership role. Daniels takes scientifically based behavior research and applies it to the workplace to cut through so much of the fluff and opinion that are found in softer management books.

family backgrounds, languages and cultures, and fears and needs, all command the attention of the same nurse. Stress, burnout, bad knees, and a blown back will force early retirement long before a repetitive motion injury will.

From a leadership perspective, it is orders of magnitude more difficult to manage a hospital than it is to manage a manufacturing floor. It is no surprise then that the management practices forged in a manufacturing environment, refined in the 1950s in the university, and deployed ever since in hospitals everywhere, are starting to break. The good news though is that by rethinking your management approach, you can develop a system that is much more in tune with the higher demands of a hospital.

Two Leadership Tools

Most leaders naturally gravitate toward the big one. Things such as strategy development, opening new lines of business, and creating partnerships are the stuff of business schools and the subjects of MHA degrees. They are high-profile projects and key to career advancement. Yet, while important, hospitals are not suffering from lack of strategy. They are rather suffering from poor execution.

What is needed is a return to the fundamentals of hospital management. While most leaders tend to focus in improving the product, there needs to be equal attention that is placed on improving the process and the people. This does not come at the expense of product improvement but will instead enhance leadership's ability to bring new services to market. Well-run operations staffed by an empowered, engaged work force make a greater range of strategic initiatives possible.

A Lean Daily Management system will overtly bring a daily focus to the improvement of processes. It will also more subtly bring the opportunity for leaders to engage in the daily improvement of their people. For this to be successful though requires a great deal of intentionality on the part of leadership. There should, at all times, be a clear distinction whether an intervention is done primarily to improve the process or to improve the people. Leaders should spend the bulk of their daily management time improving people so that their people can in turn improve the process.

What this means in practicality is that, at the beginning, little real process improvement is done. The Lean journey will feel slow and, at times, seem to be a waste of effort if measured only by process improvement. When this happens, do not worry because it is a strong indicator that the organization is on the right path. Instead, use the cultural continuum (explained in detail in Chapter 3) to measure progress.

Volumes have been written on how leaders can develop their people. Books can, and have, been written about how to develop people in the context of Lean improvement. This chapter is not an effort to either recap or replace that body of work but rather to help explain it in nuts-and-bolts detail as it relates to Lean Daily Management.

There are two basic tools at leaders' disposal: (1) focusing questions and (2) accountability. While both have broad applications outside the context of daily management, let us look at them as they apply to the topic at hand.

Focusing Questions

Focusing questions are, in essence, the Socratic method for knowledge discovery. The goal of these questions is not to generate answers but rather to stimulate and guide thought. These focusing questions are excellent for breaking through assumptions and forcing critical thinking.

> *Why do we do it this way?*
> *What is a better way?*
> *What do other hospitals do?*
> *What can we improve?*

These types of questions also create tension. Most staff will do what they are told willingly. What they do not naturally do is to critically think and innovate their areas. As the management system is deployed, there will be a desire from the staff for clear, concise directions. They will simply want leadership to tell them what to do so that they can do it. The problem with this though is that the whole point of the system is to leverage the expertise and creativity of the staff to make breakthrough changes. This cannot be done if leadership simply tells them what to do.

Instead, the role of leadership is to force thinking. This requires spotting a weakness in the thinking of people and crafting a question to create tension to address this weakness. For instance, a common reason given for problems is a lack of staff. The problem with this thinking is that it assumes that the current staff are properly using their time, that is, they are wholly focused on patient care. This, of course, is never the case as many things interrupt patient care constantly. So, the focusing question may become,

Why are nurses pulled away from patient care?

This pulls attention away from a perceived lack of staffing, something that is not likely to be changed, to true process waste that can be addressed and eliminated.

Good questioning is a difficult but learnable skill. There is a huge difference in response to questions that initially appear to be asking the same thing. The single most important rule to remember when asking a question is to avoid close-ended questions at all costs. These questions can be answered with just a word or two and demand little thought of the person who is answering.

To understand why open-ended questioning is so important, first, understand why we so strongly gravitate to closed questions. Closed questions lead to closed answers, which are easily understandable. For instance, if you ask a staff member, "Are you enjoying this Lean Daily Management process?" you are going to receive one of two answers: "yes" or "no." These answers are easily understood and require little effort from you or the person who is answering.

However, the answers are also deceptive. You will receive little actual information from that question. If, instead, you ask, "What has been good about Lean Daily Management?" you now force the person to think before answering the question. There are now an unlimited number of answers that may come back, which will in turn require *you* to think. So, the primary reason we avoid open questions is that they require effort.

The second reason we cling to closed questioning techniques is because they are safer. As the questioner, I can control the conversation much better by asking a closed question rather than an open question. Lawyers exemplify this technique when they examine witnesses. They actively avoid surprising or new information and instead drive an artificial conversation to a predetermined outcome guilt or innocence through closed questions. That works well in the courtroom, but, if we want to engage in problem-solving, we first need to recognize that there are no predetermined solutions or objectives. Therefore, the closed question is the worst possible vehicle for achieving results.

Problem-solving requires us to become investigatory and inquisitive. Because they are thought-provoking and spark dialog between people, open questions are ideal for discovering new information and should always be the question of choice.

The defining characteristic of an excellent open question is that the answer will naturally spur multiple follow-up questions. This is the heart of the scientific process—the scientist asks, "Why does that happen?" Because the initial answer is "I do not know," the next step should not be to answer the question but rather to ask a lot of follow-up questions. Consequently, the next questions become, "What would happen if...?" These questions form the basis for the hypothesis that the scientist will then try to prove or disprove.

We want to use the same technique when we solve a problem. We know that we have asked a really good question when no one knows the answer. The crucial factor now becomes, "Can we ask the right questions to move the investigation?" At this stage, it is tempting to fall back on closed questions and begin diagnosing the problem. Resist this urge. A good question to ask at this stage is,

What do we need to learn to answer this question?

Do not be afraid to ask your directors and staff this question. It promotes deep thought on the problem. The responses from the question should be a good, solid open question that can be placed on the 5 Whys sheet and Pareto chart.

To summarize, asking closed questions shuts down thinking, stifles learning, and prevents deeper-level problem-solving. Asking genuine open questions forces thinking, fosters learning, and provides a structured way to deepen problem-solving. Open questioning is a learned skill that requires practice.

Accountability

The second tool leaders have the ability to force accountability. Without this, the system will inevitably derail. There are three levels of accountability that must be maintained: (1) leader accountability, (2) manager accountability, and (3) staff accountability.

Leader Accountability

The first key is that the leadership team must keep itself accountable. It is very easy to let laziness and disorder creep into the day-to-day operations of the hospital. Rounding must occur, on time, every day, with no exception. This means that meetings cannot be scheduled during this time. If leadership loses discipline, it will instantly be felt throughout the hospital, and the effort will become an exercise of "Do as I say, not as

I do." This is the easiest part of Lean Daily Management to get right and the easiest to drop. It is the greatest single indicator of the future success of the program though.

Manager Accountability

Because leaders are in every department every day, they will have the ability to hold managers accountable daily. Managers can be held accountable for shift change huddles, the status of the problem-solving boards, and the management of other visual controls that are implemented. A good example of this is the use of a discharge board in conjunction with a problem-solving board. Because leaders are rounding daily, they can review the current status of discharges throughout the house daily. This ensures that the system is being worked appropriately by managers, escalates problems that demand senior leaders' attention, and provides coaching opportunities to develop managers' abilities.

Staff Accountability

The final layer of accountability is holding staff accountable to participate in the process. While this is technically the manager's job, senior leadership helps immensely by putting a consistent presence on the unit, especially early in the process before habits are built. This makes it clear to the staff that the impetus for involvement originates at the top of the organization, thus giving the manager more *firepower* to compel involvement in the huddles and rounds.

There is a clear distinction that must be made between holding staff responsible for involvement versus improvement. Like the golden eggs from the goose, the improvements will indeed come, and get larger over time, but only the staff are not alienated in the process. Good leaders are constantly asking, "Where has learning stopped?" and then crafting questions to help staff through the blockage. The focus is not on the final goal but rather the next step. Leaders can hold people accountable not to know the answer but rather to search for it.

As the new way of managing becomes a habit, accountability will become increasingly easy to enforce. Managers will assume the role of enforcing staff accountability, and even that will yield to staff holding each other accountable. The most critical piece though is leader accountability. Any lapse in that area will cause tremendous, potentially irreparable, harm.

Attributes of Lean Leaders

Structuring the hospital around quality, requires that leaders become quality leaders, that is, leaders of quality. This type of leadership is different from traditional leadership. This should not come as a surprise because if Lean management is a different management philosophy from traditional management, as covered in the "Introduction" section of this chapter, then, naturally, a different set of leadership attributes will be needed as well.

First, let us recap the difference in management philosophies. The traditional management style pioneered by General Motors is profit through growth and acquisition. The management style developed by Toyota is profit through reduced waste and improved quality. Everything revolves around defect reduction. Thus, the traditional approach to people is adherence to the process, whereas the Lean approach to people is to have them improve the process. As a result, traditional leaders enforce standards, whereas Lean leaders enforce empowerment.

The difference between these two leadership approaches is fundamentally a mindset, not a different list of do's and do nots. Also, despite the mindsets being different, many of the actual actions overlap. This is the reason that the *why* behind an action is more important than the action itself. Table 2.1

Table 2.1   Traditional versus Lean Leaders

Traditional Leader	*Lean Leader*
Quality is one of many areas of focus	Relentless focus on quality
Use averages and percentiles	Set and enforce rigorous standards
Measure monthly	Measure against standards daily
Punish mistakes	Reward mistakes that are revealed
Be driven by one-offs	Be data driven
Suppress conflict	Create a safe place for conflict
Lead the change	Empower others to act
Enforce standards on management	Connect to the front line
Embody and inspire cost savings	Embody and inspire quality
Charismatic	Humble
Be financially focused	Be patient focused
Ensure voice of leadership by pushing communication to staff	Ensure voice of the patient through direct, personal contact

shows a list of attributes of traditional versus Lean leaders. The list is not exhaustive, nor is it ironclad. Instead, read it as suggestive manifestations of the underlying mindsets.

Leadership is very much an art, but it is an art that is founded on an underlying philosophy. Part of the Lean journey is to slowly understand and develop a true Lean philosophy. As that happens, the attributes of Lean leadership will naturally arise. The core of Lean thinking is to view the organization from the perspective of the customer. The next chapter deals precisely with that.

Chapter 3

Connecting with the Customer

If you're not serving the customer, your job is to be serving someone who is.

Jan Carlzon

Introduction

There has been much that was written about the importance of treating the patient as the customer, and most hospitals do this fairly well on a personal level. From an operations perspective though, the term *customer* has a much different, and more technical, definition. Understanding this difference is key to effective managing processes, because without understanding the term customer, it is impossible to generate solid metrics that are critical to truly manage your processes.

Defining the Customer

While, generically, almost everyone can agree that the customer of the hospital is the patient, how we think of that customer, changes based on our starting point. For instance, a nurse will think of the patient who is in front of them at that moment as the customer. A service line leader thinks of a certain patient population subset as being the customer. The chief financial officer may think of customers in terms of funding—self, private, or Medicare/Medicaid.

None of these perspectives are wrong. They are all useful to the person who holds them. The important point is that they are all *different.* Therefore, it should come as no surprise that when we look at the hospital from an operations perspective, we think differently of who the customer is from these other perspectives.

From an operations perspective, a customer is anyone for whom the process is designed. It is whoever is downstream from the process receiving the work that has been done by previous actors. Thus, while the ultimate customer is always the patient, there are many intermediate customers along the way. We refer to these two different classes as *internal* customers, whereas the patient is the *external* customer.

Internal versus External

In a well-designed system, internal customers channel the voice of the external customer up the line so that the entire organization revolves around delivering value for that customer. Hospitals, however, are rarely well-designed systems. Instead, they are usually highly evolved systems. The problem with processes and systems that are evolved as opposed to designed is that they tend to harbor massive amounts of waste.

The differences between the two systems are stark. Evolved systems arise from simple systems that are usually designed when they are set up. For instance, much thought goes into the design and function of a new hospital when it is constructed. Once operations begin though and the inevitable problems arise, there is usually no coordinated response to them. Each nursing manager solves the problems on their floor as they arise. Support departments adjust on an ad-hoc basis. The system evolves in response to the external stimuli.

This process continues at a subdepartmental level, and staff begin to evolve their own way of working. Variation creeps in to the processes. Inconsistency becomes commonplace, and downstream units notice shifting inputs. For instance, sometimes, patients in the ED have IVs placed in the elbow rather than the wrist, complicating inpatient stays or requiring a restick. From the ED nurses' perspective, this is simply the way that they always place IVs because it is faster. They have evolved their way of working largely ignorant of the impact downstream.

Now, consider this type of evolution across the entire system. There are innumerable mini-processes, all of them changing all of the time. While this system is responsive to changing needs and maintains a degree of agility, it is also impossible to optimize because a systems-level view is lacking from those who are evolving the processes the most—the front line. Some attributes of evolved versus designed systems can be seen in Table 3.1.

Table 3.1   Evolved versus Designed Systems

Evolved	Designed
Local optimization	System optimization
Fixes shift problems	Fixes solve problems
Assumed causes	Traced causes
Obvious solutions	Nonobvious solutions
Blame the people	Blame the system
Reactive	Static
Responsive	Bureaucratic

Whereas a designed system promotes system efficiency, an evolved system promotes local efficiencies. For example, a nursing floor will flex down on their staffing with little awareness or concern for the impact on wait times in the ED. EHR systems often require the same information to be entered multiple times due to overcustomization, which breaks the data flow. Because units cannot clearly see the upstream and downstream effects, their actions have optimized what they can see—their immediate area. As a result, errors and delays abound; their true cause is hidden.

Yet, evolved systems are not without their strengths. Staff engagement is difficult in a designed system because staff empowerment so often collapses into an evolving system again. As many traditional process improvement departments are slowly learning, project implementation is very difficult if not impossible when staff are not engaged. The reason is that at the end of the day, staff own the process. So, the question becomes not how to transition from evolved to designed, but rather how to blend the two together to maintain their strengths. The idea is to blend local evolution with system-wide daily design, with the vehicle being the plan–do–study–act (PDSA) cycle. A local solution can be tested, and the system-wide impact is tested. This works because the problem is not that staff are too empowered but that they lack a system-wide view of the impact of their changes.

Value Add versus Non-Value Add

As your functional areas begin to reorient themselves around their downstream customers, they will be able to distinguish value-adding steps from non-value-adding steps. Elite organizations have a very tight understanding of where the line between value and waste lies and are able to use this understanding to streamline from the bottom up by removing operational waste.

This stands in contrast to the top–down method that most hospitals use to try to trim waste. The top–down method is a financial approach to cost reduction. A cost reduction target is set for the organization and then trickled down to the departments. Each department tries to find ways to operate within this constrained budget. A good example of this is the percentage of allowable overtime. An organizational standard is set uniformly without regard to the drastically different levels of variation in demand throughout the house. While this looks good on paper, and may indeed deliver short-term gains, there are glaring deficiencies to this approach.

First, this approach forces each department to fend for themselves. Environmental services are, for instance, incentivized to understaff shifts as much as possible, and nursing units are incentivized to operate below their budget by trimming staff. This results in severe operational deficiencies that may not become evident for many months in the form of patient satisfaction scores, quality metrics, or other operational metrics. By that time, management is convinced that the new staffing level is appropriate. By the time these problems surface, the new staffing levels are considered normal, and management instead blames the remaining people.

In the end, the hospital attempts to manage its operations with financial spreadsheets that have little relation to the actual operational realities. This makes cutting easy because the value is seen, whereas the cost of cutting is hidden. Or, conversely, if management recognizes that there does need to be improvement, they have no guidance as to where precisely additional resources are needed. This results in a yo-yo effect of downsizing and rightsizing, which serves nothing but to erode the overall experience of the work force as knowledgeable staff leave, and new hires fill their places on the next upswing and traumatize those who survive each wave of cuts.

There is a better way to manage operations. Only two questions need to be asked:

1. What are we doing that is producing value?
2. What are we doing that is not producing value?

These two questions, at first glance, seem simplistic. After all, who would continue doing something that produces no value? And, even if he or she did, how much time could that possibly claim?

What these two questions get at is that we often confuse busyness with productivity. Without understanding the difference between the two, we are doomed to simply do more of both, faster, with fewer resources. This is a losing proposition.

If, though, we can tease out what must be done from that which we do not have to do, we have the opportunity to produce more output with less effort. For example, during medication pass, a typical nurse may spend roughly half of his or her time working very hard on activities that produce absolutely zero value. While this can be difficult to detect for an untrained observer, looking for the following activities will reveal the waste that is hidden inside this nurse's day (Figure 3.1).

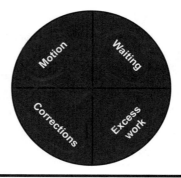

Figure 3.1   Four activity wastes.

- *Movement*—the physical walking, transportation, and motion that staff, patients, and supplies do. Examples include the following:
  - Walking between patient rooms and the medication room
  - Searching for medications
  - Clicking through the medication screen
- *Waiting*—any time that a patient is waiting for care or a care provider is waiting to provide it. Examples include the following:
  - Waiting for other nurses to pull medications
  - Waiting for a physician to return a phone call
  - Waiting for a specific medication from the pharmacy
- *Corrections*—fixing problems that are caused by earlier steps in the process. Examples include the following:
  - Needing to call a physician to clarify poorly written orders
  - Returning to the supply closet for forgotten supplies
- *Excess work*—work that is really not necessary or that should be done elsewhere. Examples include the following:
  - Mixing medication
  - Multiple log-ins to the medication machine

Together, these activities for the 4 activity wastes* ultimately impact employee satisfaction, quality, and financial performance.

These activities conspire to rob the nurse of his or her time. There are a few critical observations to make about these wastes. First, none of them involve direct patient care. In theory, we can reduce this activity without impacting patient care. From the patient's perspective, these activities are

---

* These 4 activity wastes are a simplification of the 7 process wastes that are commonly taught in Lean courses. While the 7 process wastes are more technically correct, they are often cumbersome when used in a hospital setting.

pointless and detached from why they are there. They distract from patient care. Second, these activities are natural aggravators of the nurse. Finally, none of these activities deliver financial value to the bottom line yet sap resources. These observations form the basis of the *Law of Interconnected Waste*.

Law of Interconnected Waste

This law states that all the process waste of an organization manifests itself in three ways:

1. Reduced value to the customer
2. Reduced satisfaction to the employee
3. Reduced profit to the company

This law offers some very powerful results from attacking waste. First, one of the best ways to increase value and quality is not to spend more money but rather to eliminate the waste and friction in your processes that sap value during production. Second, eliminating process waste will increase profits by reducing expenses.* Third, reducing process waste will increase the happiness of employees. This final point is vitally important to the success of a Lean management system (Figure 3.2).

Taken together, these three points reveal that there is natural alignment among employees, patients, and finances. We can leverage this natural alignment by tapping in to the current frustrations that our people have regarding the workplace. Thus, one of the best places to start when seeking to eliminate waste is to simply ask your staff,

---

* There may very well be an increase in demand and quality. That, though, is more of a marketing issue. The key observation here is that it costs money to produce waste. Any reduction in that waste results in less money that is spent on producing it.

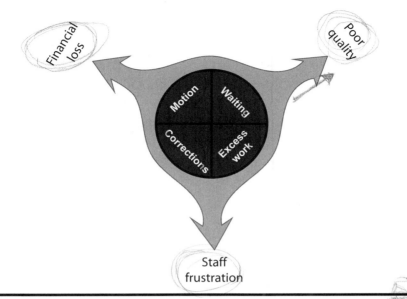

Figure 3.2   Law of interconnected waste.

What frustrates you about your job?

Any frustration they have about the daily operation of their job will invariably lead back to a process waste that impacts patients and drains resources. The management system you build will be able to take these raw frustrations, convert them into hard metrics, and then use the scientific PDSA* problem-solving to drill down to the root cause.

This is the secret to gaining employee buy-in. By tapping in to the simple fact that people prefer to do the job that they were hired to do, and that, all else being equal, they prefer to do it well as opposed to poorly, you can leverage their expertise to sniff out waste from the bottom up. Also, because your staff are constantly connected to the customers, they will naturally steer the organization back toward a customer-centric model because, like a horse that naturally follows the path

---

* PDSA, short for *plan–do–study–act*, is the core of any Lean Daily Management system and is covered in depth at the beginning of Section II of this book: Implementation.

since walking is easier, they prefer to be highly productive with lots of patient contact because that is why they entered the field in the first place.

Key Processes versus Supporting Processes

Manufacturing organizations are built around the primary manufacturing line both organizationally and physically. This is so easy to do in that environment that it is considered to be self-evident. If an untrained observer was to walk onto the manufacturing floor of a well-run company, he or she would quickly be able to identify the main assembly line. He or she would also be able to differentiate that between the supporting, or feeder, lines that supplied the main line. Finally, it would be clearly obvious that the main line should never stop; otherwise, the entire factory is not producing anything.

This is much harder to do in healthcare though because there are so many different *assembly lines*—i.e., avenues of care—that it is impossible to reorganize around just one. Most observers, trained or otherwise, have a very difficult time identifying process flows in hospitals. This is because the work is hidden and much more complex than that which is found in a manufacturing environment.

What we can do though is to borrow the thinking and adapt it to our needs. We perform this by identifying our key processes and differentiating them from our supporting processes. Simply put, key processes are those that directly touch the patient, whereas supporting processes are those that deliver what the key process needs to be successful.

An example of this can be seen in the OR. The key process is the actual patient flow. The supporting processes are the supply process, the cleaning process, scheduling, and so on. Separating the way we view these processes allows for a different way of managing them.

In an impossibly perfect OR process, the patient would physically stop except for a quick set of vital signs, starting the IV, and, of course, the surgery itself. This can be considered the main line. The goal of improvement in the OR should not be room or block utilization, or room turnover time, or inventory reduction, or any of the other common metrics that are used. While these are important, often, improving one comes at the expense of the other. For

in   block utilization rate
w   onstraint. When this
is   pre-op and fixate or
tu   eating a blockage in
p   around. Supply levels
a   eats out *just-in-time*
th   driving up the oper-

                          effort is on the sup-
p   careful eye on the
n   rough the OR. This
i   nistrators. Why do we
p   e ED as a key metric
b

                          esses are not equal,
y   e. Key processes are
t   length of stay and
l   t financial overhead.
                          to the flow of the key
                          from an operations
                          ancial gains often have

                          automotive manufactur-
                          rmine that the best way
                          er, top–down analysis
                          labor. Therefore, the
best way to   ce the headcount. The
decision is turned over to the floor operations manager.

The floor manager looks at his operations and quickly realizes that laying off assembly workers will not work. Therefore, the easy candidates are among the support staff. He makes the decision to lay off the inventory supply people. After all, those working on the assembly lane can get up and obtain their own parts.

Day 1 of the new financial improvement kicks off. Everything is running smoothly. Granted, the line started a touch later than normal as operators had to first stock their areas. They have no worries though since they know that the delay will soon be worked out. However, after nearly an hour of smooth operation, the line stops, and an eerie silence grips the shop floor. The operators have run out of parts and run off to resupply.

Eventually, the line kicks back up, and things run smoothly. Yet, soon, the line is down again, and more operators are off running to resupply their stations. This process continues with the gap between downtimes steadily decreasing and fewer and fewer operators running off to resupply at a time. The experiment is not working.

The operations manager brings the CFO out to review what is happening. The CFO quickly realizes the problem with eliminating the positions and immediately corrects it by opening up the position to new hires. Yet, the damage is done as the new batch of recruits have significantly less experience than the group who, only recently, were laid off.

The problem in this story is that management did not understand the importance of keeping the key process continuously running. Of course, this story is a bit silly in the manufacturing setting as they would have anticipated and corrected much sooner. It is painfully on point though in the hospital setting because the work is hidden, and the relationships between the key processes and the supporting processes are poorly understood.

This begs the question, "How do you reduce labor costs without compromising the key processes in the hospital?" The trick is to understand that the two types of processes must be balanced and that an hour is not simply an hour.

There are three important differences between key processes and supporting processes that need to be understood by managers. First, key processes tend to have higher-skill, higher-paid labor than supporting processes. Second, gaps in coverage in key processes quickly bring work to a halt, whereas gaps in coverage in supporting processes build up first before bringing work to a halt. Third, when the work is hidden, the halts to the line are often invisible to management.

Because supporting processes are usually staffed by less skilled employees than key processes, they are an easy target for cuts because, by retaining employees with a higher skill set, the organization retains flexibility. Oftentimes, hospital budgets count the hours that are worked, not the labor dollars that are spent, so the director is incentivized to reduce cheap labor and retain expensive labor because the expensive labor can do the lower-level tasks that are left by a vacancy, but the lower-priced labor cannot do the higher-level tasks that are required. For example, given the choice between losing an RN or an LVN, the director will always let the LVN go because an RN can legally perform LVN duties, yet the converse is not true.

When support staff are cut, the operational impact to nursing is both sporadic and intense. Focused on patient care, nurses will simply suck up the additional work that pulls them off-task rather than raise the flag to management that they are no longer operating at the top of their license. This problem festers unseen as nursing time is continually sapped away into support functions. As a result, the care time for patients is disproportionately impacted at the times when the floor is busiest and, ironically, needs the most nursing time on patients as possible.*

---

* This occurs because nurses are able to compact and prioritize tasks to accommodate the most urgent. This has an upper limit though, and, as it is reached, the cracks in the process suddenly appear violently as work is increased.

This can be easily understood by imagining a factory that is producing well below its capacity. The line can stop as supplies are refilled with no problems. As the line speeds up closer to maximum capacity though, these stops create massive amounts of chaos and large delays in order fulfillment. In the same way, if the patient/nurse ratio is low, the extra work can be absorbed. But, if volumes or acuity spikes, delays in patient care are inevitable.

Finally, because the work in a hospital is hidden and not easily measured, the delays in the key processes are difficult to detect and correct. These delays may show up weeks or months later in length-of-stay averages or even a drop in patient satisfaction scores. By then, tracing the results back to the offending process can be both time consuming and difficult, if not impossible.

Balancing the resources given to key and supporting processes is critical to achieving optimal operations. Too many support positions drain finances; too few deprive the key care processes of the help that is needed to operate smoothly. This balance is often attempted using industry averages. However, this approach, indicative of the wider *management-by-averages* epidemic that grips hospital leadership nationally, ignores the critical variations that happen that are unique to your hospital. As the saying goes, "If you have been in one hospital, you have been in one hospital." The averages focus on *what* the ratio should be without understanding why. The why can only come with a deeper operational understanding of the work being done.

Understanding the differences between key and supporting processes reveals the futility of top–down cost reduction. The work done must still somehow be done. Cutting costs is not really cutting costs; it is simply spending less and hiding the results in patient surveys, lagging operational data, staff burnout and turnovers, and quality outcomes.

A better approach is to go first to your staff and ask them what can be done to contain costs. Because they are the true experts of their roles, they know where the waste is hidden. What they need from you is guidance on solving the problems that generate the waste.

As your control over your processes increases, you will be able to elevate your key processes. This elevation raises their visibility and makes their supporting processes subservient to them. By borrowing the idea of *takt time*,* or the regular steady beat that a process must operate at to meet customer demand, you can choreograph daily operations. You can prioritize key pieces of work and delay less critical work to smooth out the overall demand in the system.† While this sounds exceedingly complicated, it is fairly simple in practice and will be one of the deliverables from your management system.

Realigning the Organization around the Customer

As the pieces of your management system fall into place and the organization becomes more adept at the daily routine, a slow shift will start to put the hospital on a path of becoming even more patient-centric. The voice of the patient will begin flowing through the management system in the form of metrics, standard work, problem-solving, and work lists. Bringing these four aspects together forms the daily goals of running your management system. Metrics show the performance level; standard work shows how the performance level is achieved; problem-solving both improves the standard work and handles

---

* Takt time is the cadence that the organization needs to operate at to serve demand. On the assembly line, it is the number of parts coming off per minute; in the hospital, it is the number of patients who need to be discharged daily to maintain equilibrium.
† This is especially powerful when applied to discharges and patient flow. This is covered in detail in Section III: Production.

one-off issues as they arise; and work lists coordinate activity throughout the hospital.

Metrics

Metrics tracked by staff will initially be small and fairly insignificant to the overall hospital. As they become more skilled and begin looking downstream to gauge their effect on the overall care process, their goals will have a greater impact. As each functional area goes through this transformation, they will eventually link up to true customer requirements or to downstream metrics that do.

Standard Work

As these key metrics begin to solidify around customer needs, standard work can be built to consistently deliver to those requirements. This standard work will deliver the following benefits:

- Reduced variation in both the time that is required and the quality of outcome for key tasks
- Better management due to a clear *best way currently known* that will exist that can be used for accountability
- Streamlined training because there is a clear standard that can be used

This standard work will be developed, owned, and continuously improved by the staff. As they become more adept at developing and maintaining standard work, it can gradually be spread to the other aspects of their activities.

Problem-Solving

Like metrics, problem-solving efforts will initially be focused on local problems with little significance to the financial bottom line. These small problems are important though because, by solving them, the staff learn how to apply the PDSA scientific problem-solving methodology, and management learns how to empower the staff and coach them through the process. The next section covers staff-driven problem-solving in much greater depth and gives a tool, the cultural continuum, to gauge the cultural development of the hospital. This tool will guide the leadership team through the staff development process to speed them toward more advanced problem-solving.

Work Lists

As a daily cadence is developed and managers learn how to prioritize work, scheduled work lists can be developed. A complete example of this can be found in Section III of this book in Chapter 9. These lists can be used in many settings though to coordinate hospital-wide activities around individual patients. The result is a systemic and drastic reduction in wait times because the hospital can now deliver care in a synchronized fashion.

This chapter has been painted with very broad, very quick brush strokes. These ideas will be developed in detail in the next two parts of this book. At this point, the goal is simply to understand the philosophy of redesigning the hospital around the patients. The actual application of this is difficult and painstaking work. Few organizations have the internal talent to tackle this themselves. For those that do not have it, the question becomes, how do they find the right guide to move them through this process?

Chapter 4

Finding the Right Guide

*What I need is someone who will make me do what
I can.*

Ralph Waldo Emerson

Introduction

Developing and implementing a Lean Daily Management
system is no easy feat. While it is far better to attempt to
build one using only the people whom you have as opposed
to doing nothing, an outside resource who has experience
can greatly reduce the learning curve for the organization.
Finding and hiring these experts though can be a difficult
challenge, and hospitals often make their decisions based
upon the price or selling skill of the consultants rather than
their capabilities, simply because the hospital leadership
does not yet know exactly what it needs. While this book
will serve as a good guide to understanding what the end
result should be and how to get there, it is worth taking a
look at exactly what should be expected from any expertise
that you bring in.

A good coach should follow the *see one, do one, teach one* model. While this is a generally good model for any sort of consultant to follow, it is especially important when rolling out a Lean management system because the product is the people.

Experience

A good Lean coach will have solid, verifiable experience leading organizations through fundamental change. While his or her experience may span several industries, he or she should also have deep healthcare experience. This is because the hospital setting is very unique. Highly educated staff and physicians will not follow the lead of an outsider if he or she cannot speak the language of healthcare. The inevitable objection, "Yes, but that would not work in the hospital setting," will arise to something. When it does, the coach needs to be able to point to specific instances where it indeed has.

Coaches also need to be active. Good Lean coaches are always learning, always mentoring, and always contributing to the larger Lean community. Elite coaches are writing and publishing work, breaking new ground in the field. Whether the materials are books, articles, or speaking engagements, there should be an active effort to expand the understanding of Lean in the hospital setting. Good coaches should have solid references from the C-suite of former hospitals.

Because Lean transformation is exceedingly difficult, a good coach is dedicated to becoming a better coach. Many Lean practitioners treat Lean and process improvement (PI) in general as a stepping stone to a larger role—perhaps a vice-president, a chief operating officer, or a chief financial officer position. While this is an excellent career path that results in senior leaders who have deep Lean experience, these people are not ideal for a Lean transformation role. Someone who is dedicated to a career in cultural transformation is much better as they are the ones who are looking for better, more refined ways to propagate Lean thinking. This is not another project for them; this is their calling.

Table 4.1 gives some positive and negative attributes of Lean coaches. Like the attributes for Lean leaders that was shown in Table 2.1, this table lists some manifestations of an underlying philosophy. Very few coaches will be able to exemplify every positive attribute, and fewer of those will successfully avoid every negative attribute. This table though is a good guide to help you rank potential coaches.

Table 4.1   Attributes of a Lean Coach

Positives	Negatives
Outside the organization	Part of the current culture and establishment
Actively writing	Minimal activity in the Lean community
Focused on training	Focused on sales
Focused on cultural transformation	Focused on projects
Prove results in the short term	Promise results over the long term
Simplified explanations in plain English	Technical jargon and Japanese terms
Clear exit point	Indefinite commitment
Transformational experience	Project management experience
Associated with a university or other credible organizations	Unaffiliated, independent, self-created methodology
Actively mentoring and coaching previous clients	No connection with previous clients
Asks questions	Gives answers
Simply explain the problem	Explain a complicated solution

Questions to Ask

When interviewing potential coaches, there are some good questions that can be asked. These questions will help sort through the sales presentation and drill down to better judge the true substance of the coach.

Who Have You Helped Recently?

This question is designed to judge activity. Because healthcare changes at a breakneck pace, not staying involved for just a few years can quickly become obsolete. Good answers should show diversity by title, help peers and people outside their contracted work, work with local universities and mentor students, and assist former clients.

How Many People Have You Coached and Trained?

Here, the higher the number, the better. You cannot transform an organization without training and coaching hundreds of people. While the depth of the involvement with the bulk of them will be shallow, it shows that the effort permeated the organization. So, a good answer here will be in the thousands.

If the answer is a couple of hundreds or less, this indicates that there was a heavy focus on project work, not a Lean transformation. Here, the coaching is deeper and more comprehensive but does not permeate the organization.

What Type of People Have You Taught and Mentored?

Answers to this question should include C-suite, managers, and frontline staff. There should be a mix of clinical and nonclinical roles. Finally, there should be some mention of developing the person who managed the program when the coach left the hospital.

What Environments Have You Rolled Out Management Systems In?

The wider the range, the better. For-profit and not-for-profit experiences are good, as are academic settings. Clinics tend to pose unique challenges, so experience there is valuable as well. Finally, if your hospital is a union shop, experience in dealing with a union environment is highly preferred.

Where Can I See Your Writing?

Do they have a website or blog, or have they been featured on other websites? Some may have books, articles, or presentations that are available online. Is the writing sustentative and detailed or mostly fluff? Is it focused on educating or selling services?

When Can I Expect You to Leave?

This should not be a permanent partnership. A good coach will have a solid understanding of what a reasonable timeline should be. It may very well differ from the suggested timeline that is given in this book, probably with very good reason. If it does, ask clarifying questions to understand the difference.

How Do I Know If You Have Been Successful?

Your coach needs to have a clear idea of what success looks like. Agreeing to that sets a common point to move toward. Also, this can be broken down to yearly and monthly targets so that you will know if your Lean deployment is on track.

How Do You Develop Yourself Professionally?

Continuous improvement is not only for organizations. It is crucial for Lean practitioners as well. Reading books and articles, networking with other Lean professionals, and attending seminars are all ways that good coaches sharpen their saw.

Who Are Your Coaches?

Every coach has a mentor. Good mentors never retire from their students. This is important because, when you hire the coach, you are also tapping into the collective wisdom of those mentors who are dedicated to the coach's success.

What Is the Next Step in Your Learning?

Good coaches are always learning. Because each hospital is so unique, there is a near-infinite number of facets, large and small, to master. Asking this question can help you understand where your coach may be deficient and allow the team to craft a strategy to compensate. Everybody is weak at something, and Lean coaches are no exception.

Site Visit

Most potential coaches will offer a site visit. This is a good chance for the leadership team to meet them and form an opinion. Some preliminary training may be offered as well in the form of a workshop. The cost of this workshop, if any, should be negligible as it is primarily a tool that the coach will use to pitch their services.

In addition to giving both parties an opportunity to meet and get a sense of each other, a site visit with a workshop also gives the leadership team a peek into the teaching style and effectiveness of the coach. Does his or her approach and demeanor work well in the culture of the hospital? It is nice to know the answer to this question before long-term commitments are made.

Time Commitment

A good general rule of thumb is that it will take three years for a hospital to fully implement a Lean management system. Whoever is brought on board to guide the hospital through this process should be able to commit to this length of time. The work will require heavy support in the beginning and will gradually taper off as the rollout progresses. By the time *hoshin* is deployed, the time commitment from the coach may be down to a handful of hours per month.

The total time to fully deploy a Lean Daily Management system will be roughly three years for a single hospital of typical size, complexity, and leadership strength. As the number of hospitals in the system increase, this three-year number can be thought of as time per hospital. A good rule of thumb is that each additional hospital will take an extra year as the coach must stagger the deployments. For hospital systems, it is advisable to phase out the outside coach and let internal resources step into the role. This will allow the hospital system to continue developing its system on its own as it now has expertise among its ranks (Figure 4.1).

This timeline is a rough estimate of the time commitment that is necessary. During the implementation though, it is

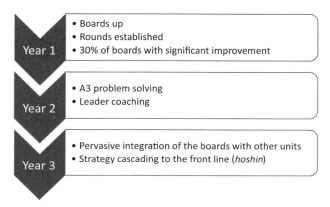

Figure 4.1   Yearly milestones.

important to go slow in order to go fast. It is very easy to outstrip the organization's ability to change and wind up alienating units and leaders. Your coach will need to pay exacting
attention to the pace of change. If he or she recommends
slowing down, heed his or her warning. Too slow is faster
than too fast.

Frequency

As mentioned in the previous section, the time commitment
required will diminish as the rollout matures. The first few
months will probably need full-time support as key habits
are formed in the organization. The activity level at this stage
is high as classes are underway; new boards are built; new
routes are stood up; and regular rounding, unit huddling, and
morning meetings are established. Your Lean coach will have
a full-time job at this stage.

As the hospital settles into a rhythm, usually a few months
in, you will only need your coach maybe two or three out
of four weeks. There will continue to be new boards and
possibly new routes that are set up, but the hospital should
have an identified person who will *own* the Lean program,
and who can handle the program largely autonomously, once
the coach leaves. Now, the coach can begin working on the
system to help make improvements in key areas. This will
involve a lot of time with frontline staff and managers who
are both on the floor in quick huddles and small, hour-long
kaizen meetings.

As the focus turns toward strategy development and
deployment, the time spent on the site may drop to just a few
hours a month as the coach checks in with the senior leadership to review progress. The coach will also spend time with
the Lean owner whom they are training to make sure that
they and the overall program are continuing to develop.

Staff Development

Getting a good coach is not about establishing a permanent relationship but rather about getting the best advice and coaching that are available. Because the exit strategy for your guide is the development of your staff, finding the right fit is important.

If your hospital has an existing PI group, a plan will need to be developed on how that group will function in the Lean Daily Management system. Usually, the Lean owner whom the coach trains to run the system will be part of that department. There can also be more than one owner depending upon the size and complexity of the initiative. Larger questions though, such as what the project work looks like once the management system is functioning, and how training needs to be modified, will need to be teased out. It is a good idea to have a general direction established before beginning the rollout and then allowing the coach and the PI team to figure out the details as the implementation is underway. This will give the PI team ownership in the new management system as well as retain the work and progress that they have made.

There should be a heavy emphasis for the coach to develop staff at all levels of the organization. Because the organization is too large for a single coach to reach everybody though, they will need to deeply develop at least one person. This person can be thought of as the *coach-in-training*. Not only will they be responsible for the management system when the coach leaves, but they will also act as a force multiplier while they are there. By training up the future coach, the external coach can keep better tabs on what is going on. For instance, while the external coach is training staff, the coach-in-training can be rounding or observing huddles. Like any other learned skill, this hand-off should follow the see one, do one, teach one model.

Exit Strategy

The formal relationship between the hospital and the coach is temporary. As such, a solid exit strategy should be part of the opening negotiations. Total engagement length, clear metrics of success, and an internal coach to be trained should be part of the exit strategy. Also, guidance around what support after the coach has left if the hospital needs additional help should be addressed. A good exit plan will clarify expectations and help ensure that the engagement with the coach ends on a positive note.

Cost

Typically, a Lean coach will charge $250–350 an hour, plus travel and accommodation expenses if necessary. A total engagement should require roughly 1750 hours, bringing the total to $437,500–612,500 over the course of three years plus expenses. While the cost of an external coach is indeed high, it is roughly in line with what hiring an experienced full-time Lean coach will cost. Annual salaries for comparable experience will be $160,000–220,000. So, the cost over three years will be $480,000–660,000. Of course, following this route will allow the hospital to utilize more of the coach's time and may be a better value. Additional costs for boards and materials can run between $30,000 and 50,000 depending on the size of the hospital and the quality of the material that is used.

IMPLEMENTATION

No great thing is created suddenly.

Epictetus

Pick up a pen and write your name. Now, switch hands and try again. Two things happen. First, the effort required to do the task goes up, and, second, the results diminish because you are writing the exact opposite way that you have your entire life.

Implementing this new management system will feel much the same way. You understand the need for it, and you can see the end goal, yet the mechanics of actually doing it will feel clunky. The reason is that success demands that you unlearn old habits and replace them with new. Your entire leadership team will feel this at different times, and frustration is an inevitable by-product. The good news is that by simply sticking with it, the awkwardness will fade. As new instincts for handling issues begin to take over, the process becomes increasingly easy.

As you read through this section on the mechanics of how to actually do this, be aware that learning them in theory is easy—they are deceptively simple. Putting them into practice though is much more difficult. To ease the process, implement the system in as small of steps as possible. Because the system is simple, the temptation is to do everything at once. Without expert guidance, this is ill advised. Instead, go from slow to fast and trust the process.

Lean Daily Management (LDM) runs on the plan–do–study–act cycle, known as the PDSA cycle (Figure SII.1). This cycle is used to prevent bias from seeping in by keeping the focus on data-driven problem-solving. Because so much problem-solving is currently done based on hunch and intuition, it will feel unnatural to *waste* time gathering data. Have the patience to do it right though because, so often, common sense turns out to be wrong.

The steps in the PDSA model are as follows:

- *Plan*—Start with a question, or hypothesis, of what might be driving a problem. For instance, if the problem is the length of time that patients wait in the ED for a bed, the hypothesis might be that it varies by floor.
- *Do*—Run the experiment by collecting data. For every fallout—in this case, a patient waiting over a certain amount of time—gather the floor that the patient is waiting for.
- *Study*—Evaluate the data to see if there is a trend developing. Once one area stands out, you are ready to take action.

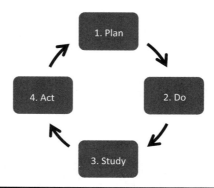

Figure SII.1   Plan–do–study–act cycle.

■ *Act*—Find out why that particular floor is driving the majority of delay. This will involve asking another question and repeating the PDSA cycle.

When a traditional Lean or Six Sigma organization first encounters LDM, there is an initial hesitation to implement LDM because they have made a significant investment into the current structure. There is an existing hierarchy of training, projects following a management format (usually define–measure–analyze–improve–control [DMAIC]), a method for reviewing and selecting projects, and an established way to track return on investment. With so much effort and work put into the system, there is a reluctance to abandon it or even to upset the status quo.

This concern reflects a lack of understanding how a Lean management system works in harmony with a more traditional Lean or Six Sigma approach. LDM brings continuous improvement to the more disruptive process improvement (PI) approach that is currently being used. Done well, the strengths of both approaches can be leveraged to cover their respective weaknesses. There are three major benefits that a Lean management system can bring to an existing program that is traditionally lacking:

1. Staff engagement around small problems
2. Identification of potential projects
3. Sustainability of projects

Together, these three benefits help backfill the current program and close the gap that is created by overbuilding a PI program without having the management system in place to support it.

1. *Staff engagement around small problems*
   Frontline staff are often absent in most PI programs. Because they are hourly employees, pulling them off the

floor for training or project work triggers a charge that hits the budget. While the wisdom of this objection is dubious, it nevertheless poses a challenge for most organizations. As a result, solutions are developed not by the people who do the work but rather by those who are removed from it. The solution is then pushed down by fiat for the front line to execute. Not only does this disenfranchise the staff, but also it jeopardizes the project.

LDM helps bridge this gap by engaging staff around problems that are within their scope to fix. By focusing on what the staff perceive as problems, engagement naturally happens. Another benefit is that PI now becomes continuous improvement. Small improvements are made every day to fix the myriad small problems that create organizational friction, making it easier to run larger PI initiatives.

2. *Identification of potential projects*

Opportunity often lurks hidden in the daily activities of the hospital. Because they are the closest to the problem, staff are the best positioned to identify these opportunities. As they chase down problems that prevent them from delivering care, these little problems will unearth large problems through the consistent use of the 5 Whys. When this happens, these can be elevated to the PI team that is to be addressed with more rigor—usually the DMAIC process or an A3. Continuous improvement runs into a barrier and becomes PI.

3. *Sustainability of projects*

One of the greatest challenges traditional PI projects face is the sustainability of the solution. Because natural variation is so high in the hospital, it is difficult to develop an ideal solution that works all the time. By integrating the sustainability plan into the daily management boards, the key performance indicators (KPIs) from these large projects can be converted into metrics that can be tracked and, if necessary, improved, by the staff, weeks or even months after the project has officially ended. In this instance, PI morphs into continuous improvement.

While it is advisable to start with an LDM system and then build a traditional program later as more complex problems arise, starting with the traditional approach does not mean that the current progress must be sacrificed. Because a healthy PI program will include both process and continuous improvement, having one does not preclude the other. On the contrary, both should be built in tandem; otherwise, one starts to outstrip the other. In a heavily traditional approach, projects stall, and training yields little impact resulting in frustrated leadership. In a heavily LDM approach, problems are uncovered that daily PDSA cannot solve resulting in disenfranchised staff. When these two approaches are combined together though, problems are identified, solved, and sustained in one integrated system.

Chapter 5

Engaging the Front Line

*Regard your soldiers as your children, and they will
follow you into the deepest valleys; look on them as
your own beloved sons, and they will stand by you
even unto death.*

Sun Tzu

Introduction

LDM begins and ends with the front line. Without their
involvement, the entire system becomes an exercise in futility.
Fortunately, gaining staff engagement is not difficult. While,
typically, employee engagement has been treated as an arcane
practice, LDM gives you a system to diagnose not only where
engagement is flagging but also why. By treating poor engagement as any other problem that can be diagnosed, treated,
and cured, staff engagement can move out of the murky
world where it currently resides in and become another measured, systematically improved metric that can be managed.

Administrator Expectations

The core expectation of LDM is that every administrator devote approximately 2 hours every day to staff development and problem-solving—1–1.5 hours to work on the hospital instead of in the hospital. While, at first, this may seem like an unsustainable commitment, there are two factors that help to achieve this. First, LDM activities will replace several activities that currently consume the administrators' time. Second, as the myriad small problems that constantly pull administrators away from more critical work diminish, the time available for doing what matters will increase. For instance, afternoon firefighting to get patients out of the ED and onto the floor can be replaced with daily preemptive discharge huddles (Figure 5.1).

Communication Structure

There are three major communication cycles that are part of the LDM process: (1) staff/administration, (2) administration/ director, (3) and director/staff. Each has specific goals and guidelines that should be in constant consideration. All three communication cycles have one all-encompassing goal: to facilitate the development of these three groups of people (administration, directors, and staff) by identifying where in the process the learning has stopped (Figure 5.2).

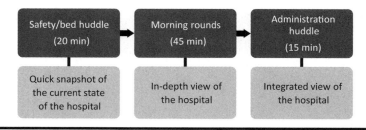

Figure 5.1 Sample daily flow for administrators.

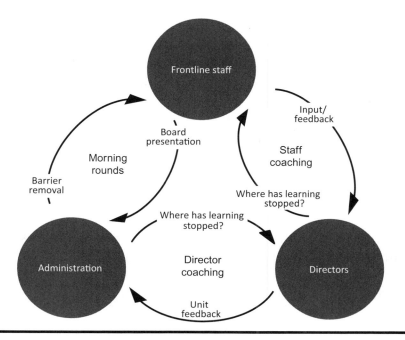

Figure 5.2   Communication structure.

Staff/Administration

This cycle begins daily at the board during the morning rounds. While the staff is responsible for having the metrics on the board updated, administration is responsible for showing up on time and listening with an open mind. Cooperation and respect result when both staff and administration show consideration to each other by doing the following:

■ Rounding as a team
■ Not keeping people waiting—arrive on time, leave on time
■ Refusing to touch a cell phone
■ Keeping the discussion tight and focused on the problems on the board—no problem-solving

Before joining morning rounds, participants should read through the LDM cultural continuum to understand at a deeper level what their role is depending upon what is encountered at the board. This is explained in depth later in this chapter.

The staff should show good exception-based reporting. The presenter should skip metrics in the green unless there is something notable to discuss. Instead, the focus should be on the metrics in the red—in particular, what the staff are doing to better understand the problem. This presentation is covered in depth later in this chapter.

The role of administration at this stage is to ask open-ended questions and guide thinking rather than solve problems. Problem-solving is the role of the staff and directors. Administrators should make notes on any deficiencies on the board or on the staff's problem-solving methodology. The presentation at this stage is not the place to attempt coaching on these issues, and this is not the administrators' role. Instead, these observations will be discussed in the administrator/director communication cycle.

For administrators, the purpose of the daily walk is to assess learning progress and to help create an environment that is free of criticism and safe for learning. Unless it is an immediate patient safety matter, administrators should not point out problems at the presentation (i.e., an uncovered linen cart). Rather, the issue should be noted and followed up with the director postwalk. Finally, without exception, administration should ask, "What can we do to help?" The goal is to round as a servant leader.

Administration/Director

After the safety huddle, rounds, and administration huddle, administrators should circle back in person with their directors at least once every week or so. The focus of this conversation is to provide the directors with feedback on the presentations as well as to allow the directors to ask for help with problems that the teams are working on. This conversation is the administrator's opportunity to help develop the director's ability to lead the staff through problem-solving exercises. Asking questions rather than providing answers results in a true learning experience. One question that administrators should be constantly asking themselves and their directors is, "Where has learning stopped?"

As problems become more complex, the staff and directors may begin to have difficulty in finding ways to solve them. At this point, the director should ask for help. If the administrator agrees that additional expertise is required, the Lean coach can be pulled in to guide the unit. Allowing staff to work through the problem to the best of their ability first will allow them to acknowledge and embrace the solutions that are provided by the PI team and to learn from the experience.

Director/Staff

The director/staff conversation is continuous but should be centered on the board at the daily huddle. These huddles usually should happen near shift change and help pull the night shift into the process. Also, they help prepare the unit for the presentation during rounds. It is the director's responsibility to ensure that the staff are trained on the board, updating the metrics, and engaged in the problem-solving process. It is *not* the director's job to solve problems. Because the desired outcome is for frontline staff to solve their own problems, the director must learn how to coach them through this process.

There are several keys to effective coaching. They are open-ended questioning, presence, and trust. Open-ended questions give staff a different perspective on the problem and the opportunity to examine other solutions. Presence is achieved by the director showing up to the presentations every day. This shows support by giving staff undivided and undistracted attention during presentations. Together, those two pieces build trust and give the presenter confidence. As a result, a safe environment for learning is created for the entire staff.

This makes it easier for them to ask the director for help when they are stuck on the board mechanics or where to go next in their efforts to solve problems. The trust established here will enhance communication by allowing staff to feel comfortable telling the director where they feel that administrators are not adhering to the commandments, enabling the director to explore this issue with administrators and continuing the cycle.

Metrics

Staff empowerment occurs only when the metrics are chosen by staff. A good metric splits events into *go* or *no-go* categories, and tracking focuses on fallouts. The goal of the metric is to record the maximum number of times a fallout is allowed to happen. If the goal is met, the unit is green for that day—if not, the unit is red for that day.

The life of a metric does not have a time frame that is associated with it. This is to allow the problem-solving process to unfold at the proper pace. However, to avoid learning stagnation, each metric should have regular time intervals to *study* (plan–do–study–act) and ask, "What have we learned? What is our next step?" This is accomplished by having an action plan for each metric with a scheduled due date to study the results.

Empowerment and ownership are accomplished when the KPIs are selected by staff; however, it is the director's role to offer guidance in the selection process to ensure that the metric is of value to the staff. Doing a *waste walk* with staff and helping them identify the 4 activity wastes can be a useful way to solicit ideas for metrics. The wastes should not be thought of as possible metrics but rather as smoke to fire. Where there is waste, ask, "What process is creating this waste? In an ideal world, how would this process perform?"—this would be your goal.

Another useful questioning technique to pull the KPIs from the staff is to ask, "What are the hard stops in your daily work flows?" "What would be ideal?"

As the unit becomes more adept at owning their processes and solving problems, directors can begin to introduce the administration board to their staff and ask them what metrics they think the unit can help with and how.

Board Mechanics

There are a huge variety of ways to format an LDM board. When setting up the layout, there are a few points to keep in mind. First, the structure of the board should be easy to modify. As the program is built and the hospital becomes more adept at the process, the boards may morph and take on additional duties. For instance, as the staff become engaged, an idea section to capture ideas or, perhaps, key numbers that are specific to the unit may be needed. So, the board should be simple and flexible.

Second, because the boards will be hung in public areas, they should be neat and attractive. Branding the management system with its own name and logo that reflect that of the hospital is a good way to unify the boards and ensure that they fit in with the wider hospital marketing effort (Figure 5.3).

This is a sample board. In this particular hospital system, University Health in northern Louisiana, the management system was branded as the "Daily U" with the "U" pulled from the main logo. This was screen-printed, along with gray 8.5 × 11-inch boxes to aid with placement of the plastic sign holders for the sheets, onto a magnetic whiteboard. Header magnets were printed so that each metric was tied back to a specific strategic goal.* Finally, for this particular rollout, each unit developed their own name, crafted their own mission statement, and identified their internal and external customers.

---

* Strategic goals were not yet established for the hospital, so a derivation of the *cheaper, faster, better* approach used to instill private-sector thinking was utilized instead.

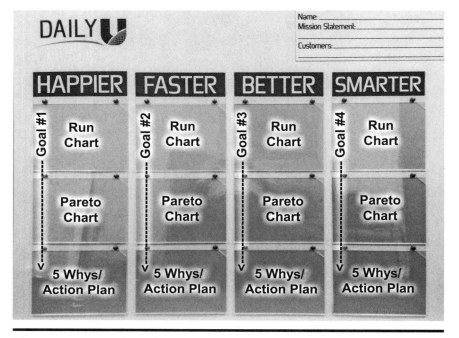

Figure 5.3   LDM board.

This information was written in permanent marker on the magnet in the upper-right corner.

Each metric covers three vertical sheets that work together to form the PDSA cycle. They are a run chart, Pareto chart, and a combined 5 Whys and action plan. Of course, templates for both boards and the sheets are available for free at LeanDailyManagement.com.

Plan—5 Whys

The 5 Whys sheet (Figure 5.4) is used to pose a question, or hypothesis, and then to drill down into the most frequent causes that are listed on the Pareto chart. Note that the questioning process may take several weeks before arriving at a genuine root cause that can be corrected.

When conducting the 5 Whys, it is important to let data drive the process, not opinion. The 5 Whys cannot be done

Fallout:_____   Unit:_____

5 WHYs (1. Plan)		ACTION ITEMS (4. Act)			
PROBLEM DESCRIPTION		Date	Action Required/Taken	Who	By When
1ST WHY:					
ANSWER:					
2ND WHY:					
ANSWER:					
3RD WHY:					
ANSWER:					
4TH WHY:					
ANSWER:					
5TH WHY:					
ANSWER:					

Figure 5.4   5 Whys and action plan.

by polling or talking, only by observing. Each new question should result in a new Pareto chart.

Do—Run Chart

The run chart (Figure 5.5) tracks the number of fallouts each day. This allows a trend to be spotted quickly and visually. Because only the fallouts are tracked, the higher the line, the more errors that were captured. This chart is a monthly chart and should be replaced at the end of each month. The old chart can rest behind the new chart so that historical trends can be seen. When actions are taken, they should be listed on the action sheet (covered in the "Act—Action Plan" section), and a vertical line with the action number above is drawn on the chart. This will help determine if the action taken was effective.

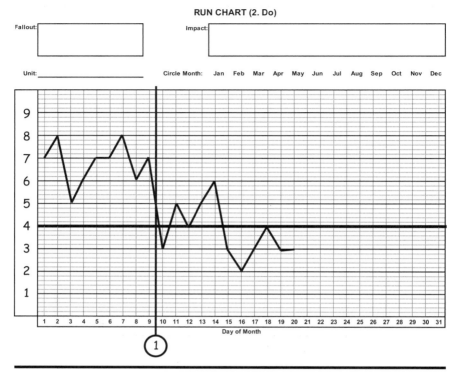

Figure 5.5 Run chart.

Study—Pareto Chart

The Pareto chart (Figure 5.6) breaks down each fallout by the most obvious root cause. This is a cumulative chart that allows the major reasons for fallouts to be discovered as the project progresses. The more frequent the occurrence, the higher the related bar will be. This chart does not rotate out every month. Instead, as the 5 Why process drills into root causes and generates new questions, a new Pareto chart will be needed.

For instance, if the question on the 5 Whys sheet is, "On which floors are ED patients waiting for beds?" the Pareto would show floors that accept ED patients. If the question shifts to, "When are patients waiting on beds?" then the Pareto would break down chunks of the day.

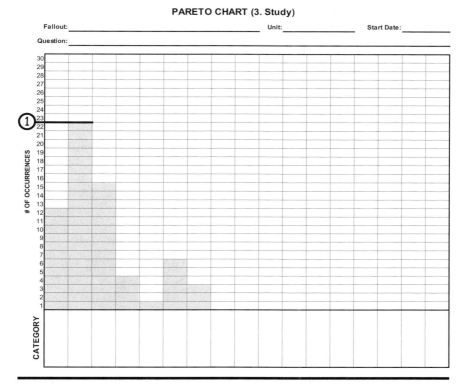

Figure 5.6   Pareto chart.

Dates should be used to populate the Pareto chart. This will allow the data to be coordinated with the run chart for auditing purposes. Once actions are taken and listed on the action plan, a horizontal line should be drawn over the bar that it is intended to affect to see if the action worked.

Act—Action Plan

As actionable items are identified, they are noted in the action plan. This action plan serves as a roll-up of all the tasks that are needed to be done to impact all of the KPIs on the board. Each action item specifies what is to be done, what problem will be fixed, who is responsible to see that it is done, and when it will be completed. Note that the action plan can include action items for people who are outside of the unit. This will happen when a supporting department is involved in the fix or when a member from administration agrees to take on a task.

Many times, an action item may simply be to continue to gather data and study the problem. This is a great use of the action plan as long as there is a time frame that is associated with this. If the date has passed and there has been no further progress on solving the problem, then questions need to be asked. Some good questions to ask at this stage are as follows:

1. Why are we still gathering data?
2. What other questions should we consider asking with the Pareto chart?

Standard Work

Standard work will be developed around the data collection process. This will increase the validity of the data and, more importantly, introduce the concept of standard work to frontline staff. The ultimate goal is to expand the concept of standard work well beyond the confines of the LDM board and out into every area of the hospital.

Usually, this standard work will be in the form of a simple tick sheet (Figure 5.7). The categories should match the categories on the Pareto chart. All that staff need to do is to make a mark whenever a fallout happens in the appropriate box. Marks can be tallied at the end of the shift, and the board is updated for the presentation.

Board Structures

Once the management system is up and running, there will be different layers of boards. The frontline boards are those that exist on the units. They can be thought of as the base of the

Question: Why are TAT > 240 min?

Reason	Occurrences
Waiting on registered nurse	‖
Waiting on MD	│
Room not available	⊮ ‖
Waiting on lab	│
Waiting on radiology	
	Blank spaces for additional reasons not yet anticipated

Figure 5.7 Data tick sheet. TAT, turnaround time.

pyramid. The top of the pyramid is the administration board. It provides a house-wide view of problems and helps guide discussions around the larger goals of the hospital. Depending upon the size of the hospital, there may be a middle layer of director boards. It provides directors a daily view of their span of control (Figure 5.8).

Boards may push data up to layers that are above them and will eventually be able to exert influence down to boards that are below them. These concepts are covered in the rest of the

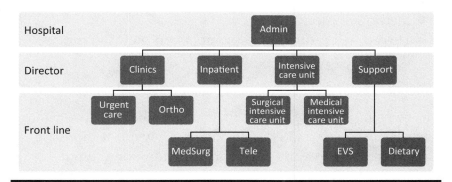

Figure 5.8 Board structures.

book. For the moment though, do not worry about the link-
ages between boards. During the early stages, it is desirable
that each board operate independently until the hospital as a
whole is comfortable with the process.

Roles

Because LDM has a specific cadence, it is necessary to have
defined roles. Much frustration happens early in the process
before people understand what their role is and have the trust
to work as a team. Defining the roles upfront will help mini-
mize this frustration.

Staff

The staff are responsible for the daily problem-solving and the
gathering and reporting of metrics. Because they are the closest to the patient, they also control what metrics are chosen.
They are the rubber that provides traction to the process.

Responsibilities

- Gather metrics daily
- Problem-solve daily
- Daily presentation to administration during rounds
- Metric selection
- Help develop other staff members on the LDM process

Directors

Directors are the *glue* that holds LDM together. They form the
link between staff and administration. They are responsible
for the state of problem-solving and learning on the unit as
well as the training and engagement of the staff in the LDM

process. They are ultimately responsible for the department's problem-solving progression.

Responsibilities

- Daily huddles around the LDM board
- Attend the morning presentation
- Drive progress on each metric
- Guide the unit toward alignment with the administration board
- Coach their staff on problem-solving
- Update the administration board
- Report out the board to administration
- Develop facilitation skills for conducting *kaizen* events, LDM training workshops, etc.
- Validate data, dashboards, and other printed reports by going to the unit and directly observing the process and its challenges
- Set departmental target conditions

Administration

Administrators are responsible for setting the priorities of the hospital with the administration board and for the development of their directors. They provide the discipline and accountability to keep the program running.

Responsibilities

- Establish five key priorities for the hospital to improve
- Walk daily on the morning routes
- Set a healthy *red-is-good* mentality at the presentations
- Create space for the staff to learn through improving
- Coach their directors on problem-solving and leadership
- Attend the daily report-out of the administration board

- President holds administration accountable for learning stagnation at the units
- Hold directors accountable for learning stagnation
- Periodically participate in frontline staff and departmental coaching sessions and daily huddles to assess/develop the director's coaching skills
- Ensure that learning and reflection take place

Morning Rounds

Daily morning rounding by leadership is the single most critical aspect of LDM. These rounds help fulfill several needs. First, it gets leadership out of the office to where the work happens. This helps them see the current state of the hospital and identify problems that need their attention quickly. Second, it helps flatten the organization by providing meaningful conversation between senior leaders and frontline staff. While there is a general acknowledgment that *rounding with a purpose* is critical, there is often little structure that is placed around those rounds to give them purpose. LDM provides just that.

Rounds should happen in the morning. Most hospitals round at 9 a.m. This is early enough that problems that are discovered can be managed throughout the day yet late enough that the floors are settled in for their shift. Whatever time is chosen needs to be turned into a no-fly zone in which no meetings are allowed to be scheduled. This is an hour of the day that is focused exclusively on working on the hospital.

Rounds should be done as a two-person team at a minimum. This is so that if one person needs to hang back, the other can continue the route so that the entire process is not delayed. This means that if your hospital has four routes, a minimum of eight people need to be available to round each day. This can usually be accomplished by having the chief executive officer, the chief operating officer, the chief nursing officer, and the chief marketing officer each take the lead on a route and directors join them. This approach also allows those directors to see the entire process and be a part of the leadership debriefing after the walk.

Round Routes

Routes should be process based. Best practice is to walk a specific value stream backwards. This will allow leaders to begin seeing problems in the process and walking upstream with an eye to what is causing the defects. This approach to route creation will facilitate problem-solving as units begin working with other units upstream and downstream, as well as when several units focus on particular hospital-wide metrics. Here are some suggested routes (Figure 5.9).

Board Presentations

The presentations themselves should last no longer than 3–4 minutes. The goal is to give a quick snapshot of the current state of the unit and where they are in the PDSA cycle. If there is nothing to report on a metric, then the presenter can skip it and move on to the next metric. Any

OR	Cardiac	Women and Children	Supporting
Med surg	Telemetry	Pediatrics	EVS
Surgical ICU	Case management	Pediatric ICU	Dietary
PACU	Cardiovascular	Nursery	Facilities
OR	Medical ICU	Neonatal ICU	Resp. therapy
Pre-Op	Cath lab	Postpartum	Lab
Registration	ED	L&D	Pharmacy

Figure 5.9   Route structure.

outstanding circumstances that the unit is facing that day should be brought up. Staff may request assistance if needed. Administration should always make a point to ask what they can do for the staff to help drive home the spirit of servant leadership.

Presentations occur at a set time every weekday. Only under extreme circumstances should a unit be allowed to skip their presentation. If that happens, administration needs to circle back after the walk and find out why.

Additional resources, including presenter scripts and rounding tips, are available at LeanDailyManagement.com.

Cultural Continuum

LDM is first and foremost a cultural development tool that operates by empowering staff through the teaching and application of Lean concepts. As such, it is important to understand that each individual, each unit, and the entire hospital develop at different rates. This cultural development can be understood as a progression through distinct phases along a cultural continuum, shown in Figure 5.10.

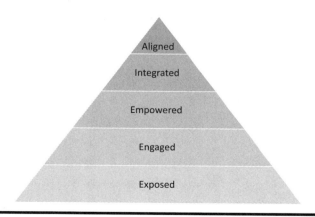

Figure 5.10   LDM cultural continuum.

Each phase is a distinct step in the learning process. As staff and units progress through these phases, their needs will change, as should the expectations that are placed on them. It is vital that units progress through these phases at their own pace. Each unit has its own cultural history and personality makeup. Any attempt to rush them to the next phase will ultimately backfire, likely spectacularly. These are phases of growth, not benchmarks to be met, and there are no shortcuts.

Exposed (Completion: Zero to Two Months)

When an LDM board is first rolled out, the unit has just entered the beginning of the exposed phase. As they progress through this phase, more and more staff will be aware of the board, having a working knowledge of how it functions, and be able to competently report out metrics. The energy level around the board may remain low in this phase because the unit as a whole has yet to embrace the board as their own. At the end of the exposed phase, the unit has been educated on LDM. A good visual indicator of this phase is the metric that is centered on the staff training of LDM. This metric, *number of staff who are not trained on LDM*, will show how pervasive the staff understanding is.

Challenges

- Staff views LDM as yet another initiative that will fizzle.
- Staff perceives LDM to be a time waster.
- Staff does not understand the benefit.

Tips for Directors

- *Hold staff responsible for receiving training.* It is very difficult for your frontline champion to both train and drive accountability.

■ *Ensure that the work around updating the board is as light as possible.* Do not update the board yourself as this robs them of ownership of the board and the data. If staff are spending more than 3–5 minutes updating the board each day, you should push them to simplify.

■ *Keep asking your staff what their frustrations are.* Help them craft metrics around those frustrations. Do not give them metrics around frustrations, but coach them through the creation of the metrics.

■ *Observe as many presentations as possible.* Provide immediate feedback to the presenter after the administrator team has moved on.

Tips for Administrators

■ *Never be late.* Show that you are serious and start and stop on time.

■ *Do not use your phone for anything, ever.* No matter who is calling, let it go to voice mail or, better yet, leave your phone in administration. Nothing communicates "I do not care" to a staff presenter faster than talking or texting. We have a no-fly zone—use it.

■ *Staff will want to explain the mechanics of the board and not the metrics. Let them.* Use this as an opportunity to gauge their level of understanding.

■ *Ask how staff chose their metrics.* This is a check to make sure that they are genuinely staff driven.

■ *Get excited about a metric.* Expound on the impact that it will have for other staff members and patients.

■ *If the presenter is poorly trained, remain supportive.* Realize that the director will use that as an opportunity to coach. Stress that this is brand new and that learning is the goal, not perfection.

■ *Ask what the staff needs from you, but be careful about saying yes.* At this point, buy-in is not the goal, and they may not know enough yet to make an intelligent request.

Implications for the Administration Board

At this stage, staff are not yet ready to help with administration metrics. Administration should continue tracking those metrics but must not push it to the LDM board. Not only is the unit early in its Lean development, but also administrators are early in their coaching development. The longer administrators wait to try to integrate the LDM boards with their own board, the better the result will be.

Engaged (Completion: Two to Four Months)

As a unit buys into the LDM system, they enter into the engaged phase. While this phase is characterized by high energy around the board, that energy must be validated before the engagement is locked in. The unit must collectively believe that they own the board and that administration is there to support them. Once this has been proven to them, the engagement becomes hardwired.

Challenges

- Staff do not trust that the board is not going to be used to punish. They believe that *red is bad* and will want to celebrate green.
- Staff will want to improve metrics instead of solve problems to keep their metrics green. This results in the *Hawthorne effect** of improvement through scrutiny.
- Staff do not believe that the board will result in supportive action by leadership.
- Staff will not be ready to do good root-cause problem-solving and will hit walls that seem insurmountable.

---

* The Hawthorne effect is the idea that people change their behaviors when they know that they are being observed. This will result in an improvement in the metric but not the process. This improvement will be short lived as old habits erode the influence of observation.

Tips for Directors

- *Begin letting go of the board as much as possible.* As the training metric nears completion, ask staff in your daily meetings what they think the group should work on next. Do not suggest a metric. Ask, "So what do you guys think that we should work on next?" and then stay quiet. If nothing comes up, try again the next day. The worst thing that can happen at this point is for you to push a metric in order to fill a space on the board.
- *Get excited when a fallout makes it to the LDM board.* Get curious about *why* and not *who.* Intentionally attempt to avoid finding out who caused the fallout. If you do find out *who,* thank him or her publicly for catching it and reporting it. Stress that the only way we can fix things is if we know what is broken.
- *If metrics are all green, get curious as to why.* Remind staff that we do not want to try harder; we want to make work easier. The goal is to create a no-blame culture around the board. Do not be aggressive with your root-cause problem-solving yet.
- *Fulfill a request.* At some point, the staff will ask you for something. Find a way to make it happen quickly. Put your name on the action plan, and encourage your staff to hold you accountable for accomplishing that task.
- *Communicate very openly with administration on the current state of the unit.* This information is incredibly helpful in preparing them for the presentation each morning.

Tips for Administrators

- *Do not ask too many "why" questions yet.* Until the staff have engaged in the process, there is a high risk that they will perceive probing questions as an attempt to find out who screwed up instead of what process problem needs to be fixed.

- *Fulfill a request.* At some point, the staff will ask you for something. Find a way to make it happen quickly. Put your name on the action plan, and encourage the staff to hold you accountable for accomplishing that task. This is the single most impactful thing that you can do to ensure that the staff are engaged.
- *Ask what you can do for the staff.* They may give you something that is completely unrelated to the metrics. If possible, run with it and make it happen.
- *Encourage local problem-solving.* If the request is something that should be handled by frontline staff, encourage them to solve it at their level. Be gentle about this though—it is better for you to pick up the slack and show action than for the staff to disengage.
- *Congratulate the green on the board, but note that red is good.* The last thing you want is for the staff to waste their time tracking stuff that does not need to be fixed.
- *Do not worry about permanent solutions.* As metrics trend toward green, be aware that it is likely the Hawthorne effect at work. Once the metric is removed, the problem may return. There is nothing wrong with this. At this stage, the goal is engagement, not improved metrics. If the problem returns, the unit will then likely be in the empowered phase and will be ready to do some digging to solve the root problem.

Implications for the Administration Board

Once a unit enters this stage, they are ready to begin helping collect data on administration's metrics. However, metrics must not be pushed down on the unit. Instead, directors should be exposed to the administration board and invited to share the problems that administration is working on with the staff. If the metric does not appear at this stage, that is likely a very good sign because it indicates that the director is allowing the unit to develop rather than pushing for results.

Empowered (Completion: Four to Six Months)

Once a unit begins doing real root-cause problem-solving, they are entering the empowered phase. The focus of the problem-solving at this point should be things within the unit that can be fixed. A unit can be considered empowered when they make processes fix themselves without asking the permission of administration.

Challenges

- *Staff typically view problem-solving as something that leadership does.* They tend to try to work at a process that is harder rather than improving the process.
- Staff will tend to get trapped in either/or thinking, i.e., the only way to improve a metric is to add staff.

Tips for Directors

- *Focus on the waste.* Either/or thinking arises from not looking at an activity as value producing versus wasteful.
- *Be aware that this phase may be a frustrating one for the staff.* Driving down to root causes and finding solutions are often a very laborious process. Keep your staff focused on easy wins. Fast beats big.
- *Foster a "forgiveness-over-permission" mentality.* When staff come to you for approval or help, push the decision back on them as much as possible.
- *Celebrate both successes and failures.* Look for teaching opportunities in every improvement that the staff attempt.
- *Maintain faith.* Know that PI is not the nice, sanitary, linear path that it so often seems to be when we look at improvements in hindsight. In reality, most of the time, answers will be fleeting, and improvements are seemingly impossible.

Tips for Administrators

- *Ask "why?" questions.* Begin developing the root-cause thinking capabilities of the staff. Use the Socratic method to guide thinking and teach problem-solving.
- *If "why?" questions are getting derailed by staffing or capital restraints, ask instead "who," "what," "when," "where," or "how" questions.* For instance, if the deepest reason found for an issue is lack of staff, try pushing through by asking, "What takes time away from the patient when you are short staffed?" By doing so, you have acknowledged the perception and returned the discussion to process issues.

Implications for the Administration Board

Once a unit feels empowered to make changes, they are ready to be challenged by the director to start working on something that tracks back to the administration's board. A good way to make this happen is for the director to take some of the staff to the board and ask them, "What can we do to impact one of these?" If the unit is truly in the empowered phase, they will run with it. Staff have a natural desire to see the hospital succeed.

Integrated (Completion: Six to Nine Months)

As units tackle more complex problems, their root-cause analysis will take them off the unit to other areas of the hospital. If this happens too early, the units are not ready to honestly and proactively share data and ideas to fix the problems, and the metric will stall. Once the units are able to share data and cooperatively use their boards to fix root-cause problems that span multiple departments, they have successfully integrated their LDM programs with the other units.

However, integration requires a high degree of trust and relationship building and cannot simply be implemented into a new area. If two units have successfully integrated with other units but never with each other, they will still have a cultural curve to overcome as new relationships are built and new trust is established. While all units will be integrated with some other unit(s) at some point, realistically, the hospital will never achieve 100% integration due to the number of units and employee turnover. Thus, the hospital will never fully exit the integration phase.

Challenges

- Units may try to work on metrics with another unit before both of them are ready. This will lead to a perception of blame or on actual blame being placed.
- Metrics may be poorly aligned or measuring different things.

Tips for Directors

- *Keep the director-to-director communication flowing.* Make sure that the units are at the same level in the process. If necessary, go visit the unit, see their board, and praise anything that is possible. Thank them for working with your team, and make sure to highlight the wins.
- *Develop a culture of owning failure and sharing success.* Encourage your team to give extra credit to the other units when presenting. Do this with your own staff as well, and ensure that they are present to receive credit.

Tips for Administrators

- *Look for consistency among the boards.* It is acceptable for the metrics to be different from board to board, as long as they are not measuring the same fallout. If they are, then the data on the boards should be fairly consistent.
- *Ensure that metrics are appropriately scoped.* Good cross-functional metrics should either measure something

internal that the unit can improve or should be a data source that the upstream unit cannot easily measure themselves. Care needs to be taken to ensure that the upstream unit does not feel like they are being collected on. Rather, they should feel that their downstream partner is gathering daily feedback for them. If the culture is not yet ready for this, discourage the metric.

Implications for the Administration Board

As units become aligned, they will be better able to take larger, cross-functional action on the hospital-wide metrics. Administrators should feel comfortable bringing directors together from a single value stream and challenging them to have their staff focus on a particular metric on the administration board. As always, the administrator and directors must never dictate what the LDM metric will be; that is for the staff to decide. However, if the targeted units are truly aligned, the staff will have no problem tracking issues across departments in a way that hits the strategic metric.

Aligned (Completion: Nine Months to Two Years)

As the hospital becomes adept at solving increasingly complicated interdepartmental issues, it becomes ready for true strategic alignment. In this phase, strategic planning can cascade down to the point that every unit knows what daily targets they need to hit to drive the organizational strategy. This phase is covered in Chapter 8.

Cultural Evaluation Tool

The purpose of this tool is to act as a barometer for the units to guide future exchanges between administration and the staff and directors. It is not intended to be used as a checklist to guide metrics or the board presentation, nor is it intended to be used as a punitive measure. Instead, this tool is an attempt to bring a measure of objectivity to the cultural evaluation of LDM and should be used as a starting point for leadership discussion, not as an end point to rank units (Figure 5.11).

When rounding with this tool, it is imperative to not let it have a chilling effect on the presenter. This tool should not be used until a route is fairly well established and a certain level of trust is built. The staff will be very aware of a member of administration evaluating them while they are present. Therefore, only one person should use this tool on a route at a time, and that person should stay on the fringes of the presentation and add positive encouragement wherever possible.

Ultimately, this tool is to help leadership evaluate where learning in the building has stopped and give some indication

UNIT	Peds	PICU	Nursery	NICU	Postpartum	L&D
EXPOSED — Staff aware of LDM	■	■	■	■	■	
Present board mechanics well	■	■	■	■	■	
Multiple presenters	■	■		■	■	
Run chart up to date	■	■	■	■	■	
ENGAGED — Celebrate the red	■	■		■		■
Positive energy at the board	■	■		■		
Focus on problems	■			■	■	
Pareto current and cumulative	■			■		
EMPOWERED — Proper use of 5 Whys	■					
Testing of countermeasures						
Unit-level process fixes	■					
INTEGRATED — Gathering data for other units						
Other units gathering data						
Downstream unit metrics						
ALIGNED — Goals tied to strategic objectives						
One metric supporting the admin board						
One metric feeding an admin metric						

Figure 5.11 Cultural Evaluation Tool. NICU, neonatal ICU; PICU, pediatric ICU.

as to why. Any other use risks alienating the staff and causing the unit to disengage.

Question Guide

Exposed

Staff Aware of LDM

Staff should be aware of rounds, the board, and the metrics that they are measuring. Some good indications of this are someone waiting for the team to arrive, a decorated board, the presence of the director, or a checklist of people who are trained in LDM.

Run Chart Up to Date

Data on the run chart should be current for all metrics up to the previous day.

Multiple Presenters

As exposure grows different, people should present the boards, either as a group or rotating from day to day.

Present Board Mechanics Well

The presenter should demonstrate a solid working knowledge of how the board functions, from the goal down to the Pareto chart. There will likely be little understanding on the functionality of the 5 Whys and the action plan. At this stage, that is fine. The learning required for the 5 Whys will come when the unit is ready for more advanced problem-solving.

Engaged

Positive Energy at Board

The unit should be happy about the rounds. Some things to look for are staff popping in during the presentation and the celebration of wins.

Pareto Current and Cumulative

The Pareto chart should be stacking up over the course of a few days. Dates should be used to fill the blocks. The number of dates on the Pareto chart should be equal to or greater than the number of fallouts on the run chart. While, initially, run charts may exhibit bad metrics, at this point, they should be tracking specific fallouts as opposed to averages or positive events.

Focus on Problems

The bulk of the presentation should be dedicated to the Pareto chart and how the root causes are being broken down as opposed to the run chart and how the unit performed the day before.

Celebrate Red

Staff should enjoy exposing their fallouts to administration. Some things to look for are good energy when talking about missing the goal or the staff mentioning that they know that there are more fallouts that they have not captured yet.

Empowered

The Proper Use of 5 Whys

As the Pareto chart shows a clear root cause that is not easily solvable, the unit should change it out with a new Pareto asking a new question. This should be reflected on the 5 Whys sheet.

Testing of Countermeasures

The action plan should begin reflecting the steps that are taken to fix process problems. Often, metrics will move without specific action that is taken. This is the Hawthorne effect and, while valuable, does not constitute true problem-solving. At this stage, the problems may or may not be fixed—the only question is whether the staff are shifting into process-focused problem-solving.

Unit-Level Process Fixes

The unit has taken specific actions that have resulted in a metric permanently shifting to green.

Integrated

Gathering Data for Other Units

Units should, on occasion, gather data for an upstream or downstream unit, either because they are in a better position to see fallouts or because they are attempting to provide better service to their internal customer.

Other Units Gathering Data

As LDM matures and organizational trust is built, units should become more comfortable asking other units to report their fallouts.

Downstream Unit Metrics

As units tackle increasingly difficult problems, multiple units should begin focusing on one issue that spans multiple areas.

Aligned

Goals Tied to Strategic Objectives

As the hospital becomes more refined in formulating strategic goals and cascading them down to the front line, the metrics on the boards should start to reflect those strategies. Note that these metrics will usually not be a direct parroting of strategies but rather developed through the catchball sessions that will be covered in Chapter 8.

One Metric Supporting the Administration Board

As the level of sophistication on the units grows, metrics should begin supporting administration metrics indirectly. There is no formal linkage, but an understanding on the part of the unit that improvements on the LDM board will result in improvements on the larger metrics.

One Metric Directly Feeding an Administration Metric

As the entire Lean program matures, the unit LDM boards should track critical problems in the hospital and feed that data to the administration board in a way that the data can be aggregated daily to provide a real-time view of hospital-wide fallouts and causes. This will enable leadership to direct problem-solving to the critical areas in an organized, cohesive manner and solve problems holistically.

While this tool is evaluating the actions of the staff, it is also measuring the capability of the management in that area. Over time, this tool becomes a leadership x-ray to not only identify the weak spots in the hospital, but also put some definition around why they are weak. This gives leadership the opportunity to intentionally develop the management capabilities of the hospital. In fact, once the system is up and running, the primary job of leadership is to develop management.

Chapter 6

Developing Management

*Command of the many is the same as the command
of the few. It is merely a question of organization.*

Sun Tzu

Introduction

There is a sharp difference between a good nurse and a good
nurse manager. It is not that one cannot be the other—it is
difficult if not impossible to be a good nurse manager without also having strong nursing skills. Hospital leaders are well
aware of this, and so the starting point to the nurse leadership path usually first requires a certain level of experience
and expertise. Experience is measured by how long the nurse
worked in which clinical settings. This language is readily
seen in resumes and job postings and is an excellent way to
determine how much a nurse has been exposed to.

Expertise though is much more difficult to quantify. Other
industries have struggled with the same fundamental question:
How do you determine the true capabilities of a person, either
as a new hire or a candidate for promotion?

This gap is especially pronounced when transitioning an experienced clinician into a leadership role, because mastery of the clinical skill set is a poor predictor for mastery of the managerial skill set. In fact, some of the skills that make an excellent clinician must be unlearned to become an effective leader. Good clinicians find ways to get the job done, usually by simply rolling up the sleeves and working harder and faster. As managers though, there is simply too much to be done to *outwork* the problems. So, while the natural instinct is to jump in and start doing the work, this is the wrong way to consistently manage a hospital floor. A new skill set and a new set of instincts are needed.

As John Maxwell points out in his book *The 5 Levels of Leadership*, people start their leadership journey as highly competent individuals. This is only the beginning of the process to become an effective leader though. While most hospitals have well-defined criteria for experience, they have few, if any, criteria for expertise especially when it comes to management. Developing a daily management system addresses this gap by converting many of the management functions into standard, repeatable daily tasks that can be quantified and therefore measured.

Developing Standard Work for Management

Healthcare is replete with *best practices* thinking. This thinking is used to develop and improve clinical procedures and establish targets for the organization. While far from perfect thinking in terms of best practices do offer a few benefits. First, it helps break through the *this-is-how-we-have-always-done-it* mentality. By forcing people to look outside the walls of their own hospital, it broadens their horizons and exposes them to new ways of doing things. Second, best-practices thinking dehumanizes the current gap in performance. This is a marked improvement from *best-people* thinking in which outcomes are based on *who* is doing the work instead of on *how* the work is done. Third, because the focus is now on the process instead of the people, there is a strong focus on process improvement that is centered on developing consistency and reducing variation. In essence, this thinking states that there is a best possible way to do something, that the secret to this lies in the process, and that any competent person can learn to do it.

Organizations that do this well apply this thinking as a starting point, not a final solution. The goal is to take work that has been artisan in nature and convert it into standard work. This work standard should be exacting, precise, and developed and continuously updated by the staff who do the work. This standard becomes a tool to both train and audit and forms the foundation for future improvement. While a detailed look into best practices and standard work is both highly important and outside the scope of this book, it is worth noting that organizations usually apply this to their staff only.

What if, though, there were best practices for management? This causes cognitive dissonance for many because management and leadership abilities are often assumed to be innate and the work itself is considered an art. Managers develop their own *styles*, and who is to say if one style is better than the other? Consider two managers: one who considers himself or herself a *hands-off leader* and the other who likes to be *in the trenches*. The approaches of these two managers are polar opposites, yet it is considered mild heresy to suggest that one is empirically better than the other.

Because we have no standard for managers, many hospitals use employee evaluations to gauge manager effectiveness. However, this actually exacerbates the problem because employees are no more qualified to identify solid leadership than the manager. While they are better positioned to see leadership gaps, they have no standard from which to base their judgments. As a result, managers are incentivized to leverage their relationships with the staff come evaluation time. This is seen when annual evaluations come around and managers rush to announce improvements that they have been saving for just this time and to remind their employees of everything that they have done for them over the past year. The scene is not unlike that of a small-town politician running for reelection.

All of this begs a very simple question: if we cannot *define* what good management is, how can we *develop* people to be ready to step into leadership? To grossly simplify the solution, hospitals must do the following three things to close the gap:

1. Create a detailed best practice for managers and leaders
2. Develop existing leaders to the standard
3. Develop future leaders to the standard

Developing Best Practices

Creating a best practice is difficult for any task. It is near-infinitely more difficult when applied to *fuzzy* skills such as leadership. The reason is that the tasks of leadership have been poorly defined. You can easily verify this by asking your managers what their daily activities are, that is, what scope of work constitutes being a manager. The answers will vary significantly, but you will be able to lump them into buckets. For instance, the following answers would be typical responses to the question:

- "I make sure that my patients are properly cared for."
- "I run my floor as efficiently as possible."
- "I support my staff both on and off duty."
- "I create the work schedule."
- "I keep my staff's credentials and training up to date."
- "I keep my doctors satisfied."
- "I handle patient complaints."

There will likely be little structure to how these tasks are accomplished. By contrast, ask an OR circulator nurse what his or her daily activities consist of, and you will get a much more concise list that is applicable across almost any other hospital. His or her response would look something like the following:

- "I arrive 60 minutes before the first case starts and make sure that the supplies have been pulled the night before."
- "I meet the patient in pre-op to get the consent signed and answer any questions."
- "I check with the physician and the anesthesiologist to make sure that we are good to go and let them know that the patient is ready for them."
- "About 20 minutes before start time, I get the OR team setting up the room."
- "About 10 minutes before start time, I go and get the patient from pre-op."
- "We have a safety stop, make sure that we are good to go, and do the case."
- "After the case, I repeat the previous steps until we are at the end of the schedule."

Notice that there is a timing to every activity. There is an expected regularity to the work. Of course, because the OR is a highly scheduled environment, it is much easier to build a best practice there than on the floor or in the ED where chaos is rampant due to highly fluctuating patient demand. The point then is not to say that all best practices should be to this level but rather that all best practices should be as close to this level as possible.

Fortunately, we have a cheat that we can use to help hospitals develop a system for their managers, their own best practice. There is a principle in statistics called the central limit theorem, which states, in a nutshell, that the more sampling and averaging you do, the more the distribution of those averages approaches a bell curve. We can use this same thinking and apply it to the day-to-day activities of managers.

This starts by rethinking the role of management. Our traditional approach has been to view managers as the catchall for whatever frontline staff cannot handle. Thus, the greater the span of control, the greater the variation in what a manager needs to do from day to day. However, this violates the central limit theorem, which states that the more variables we have, actually results in higher predictability, not lower. This is the mathematical reasoning behind Sun Tzu's insight into management by organization, and it is highly applicable to the current hospital managers.

The key insight is this: while hospital floors are chaotic, managing them does not have to be. What is lacking is a system. A good system should do the following:

- Make the current state of the floor easily visible
- Make the future state of the floor predictable
- Highlight problems before they occur
- Allocate *what* gets done *when*
- Off-load or automate mundane tasks so that focus can be placed on the truly important needs of the day

There are two questions that must be answered when building this system:

1. Is management an art?
2. Is management a science?

The answer to both of these questions is yes. Successful resolution of the tension between these two is critical to creating a management process, and it helps to look at other industries that have struggled with the same problem.

High-end automotive manufacturers have faced the same basic question. Is the car they produce a work of production and process or artistry? Like us, their answer has been *both*. The question then becomes how do they integrate both into the fabrication?

First, though, a bit of background is necessary. Ever since the Industrial Revolution, there has been a war raging between the value of craftsmanship and the efficiency of automation. You can see this clearly in the furniture industry. On the one hand, there is the mass-produced furniture from Ikea, Target, and Wal-Mart, and, on the other hand, there is the handcrafted furniture from high-end woodworkers who specialize in customization. There is little shared ground between the two sides.

Historically, both healthcare and leadership have been firmly entrenched in the craftsman camp. After all, each patient is unique and different, and each employee is unique and different as well, so, therefore, standardization does not apply. The obvious drawback to the approach is a lack of efficiency that can only come from standardization. For decades, we have been stuck at this *impasse* with no clear way forward. However, there is a third way, a method to mesh the two approaches together to reap the benefits of both, and this is clearly seen in high-end automotive manufacturing.

When building a super car, there is a relentless focus on one thing: quality. Quality is, in essence, how closely the production of the car matches the design of the car. This is a key point that these high-end manufacturers share with healthcare. In both industries, the quality of the final product outweighs the importance of the final cost of the product. What the car builders must do though is to produce a profit, and they do not have the luxury of governmental or other third-party support. Also, their product is not, strictly speaking, a necessity. There are other cheaper ways to get from A to B. As a result, they have learned how to marry efficiency with quality, and that lesson is applicable both to hospital operations and hospital management.

If the ultimate goal of a super car is quality, then the ultimate goal of each step in the production process is quality as well. This leads to a very unique production process—part of which is highly automated and part of which is reminiscent of Old World craftsmanship. The body components are formed by a machine, as this is the most reliable method to produce them, yet welded by hand because no machine can match the quality of an expert welder. Custom paints are mixed by computer and applied by a master painter because, while the machine can paint more efficiently than a human, it cannot match the quality of a well-trained craftsman. Leather for the seats and steering wheels is cut by machine but stitched by hand. The result is a machine that oozes quality and craftsmanship at a price point that commands the attention of serious buyers.

This echoes an existing principle that is occasionally heard in the hospital—that of operating at the top of one's license. Like the sports car manufacturer, your management best practice should automate that which can be done better with automation and rely on the expertise of managers for that which cannot be automated. Atul Gawande, in his famous "Cheesecake Factory" article, advocated for processes and standardization, whereas his critics decried his automated approach to delivering care to a diverse range of people. Both camps are correct, and neither is mutually exclusive. The thorny part is figuring out which parts can be standardized and which cannot.*

Now that we see what we need to accomplish, we are faced with the daunting task of figuring out how to do it. This is typical of any Lean application—the what is simple, whereas the how is murky. To help with that, let us establish a road map.

---

* When done well, Lean is about tying the long-term vision, or True North as will be covered in Chapter 7, with the current state. The result is not a clear path of sequenced steps to arrive at the goal but rather understanding what the next step should be. Lean practitioners learn to associate the murkiness and uncertainty as an indication that they are on the right track, because if it were a simple path to the ideal, the organization would have achieved that years ago.

The first point is to understand that management systems are evolved—they are not created *ex nihilo* (out of nothing). The first task is to determine what activities of managers can be automated and what cannot. Do not worry if the list of automated tasks is short. This is not the last breakdown that you will do; this is only your starting point. So, for instance, you may determine that reporting census is a good, though modest, first step. Or, if this has already been done, you may decide that determining the current discharges, or those of tomorrow, is ready to have some rigor placed around it.

In either case, the goal is to remove managers from things that they do not need to be involved in. At first, this can feel like a loss of control, but, in the end, there is a much greater degree of control. While managers usually classify themselves as being either hands-off or engaged in the details, both of these miss a much more fundamental point: what is management's highest value?

Fortunately, there is much agreement around this point. High-value managers develop their people, improve their processes, and engage emotionally with both their employees and patients and their families. So, just as we want physicians and nurses working at the top of their licenses, we also want managers operating at the highest level of their position.

A simple approach that we can use is to split activities into those that involve contact with staff and patients and those that do not. This is analogous to determining which steps are value added in a service industry by splitting them into steps with customer contact and those that are without. In this instance though, the staff can be thought of as the customer of the manager.

With this split in mind, we can now build some standard work for management. The goal of Lean is not to make the actual value-creation steps more efficient but rather to remove the waste that prevents them from getting done. The goal of management standard work is not to speed up the time that is spent with patients and staff but to free up time that is spent elsewhere. The result should be more time that is spent with patients and staff and less time putting out the myriad fires that go along with hospital management.

Implementing a Lean Daily Management system provides a good starting point for the creation of this standard because it codifies a simple, data-driven approach to problem-solving that is consistent throughout the hospital. This is done every day both during the leadership rounds and in the unit huddles outside of those rounds. Because objectives are clearly defined on the boards and progress is uniformly tracked on the action plan, managers have a system that they can use to tackle problems on their units. This best practice to problem-solving lends itself to naturally become part of a larger management best practice.

For instance, as problems are addressed and root causes found the need for shift change, huddles become more pronounced. As discharges are tracked across the hospital,* the need for a standard discharge process becomes more apparent. Because every unit now has a standard way to approach problems that span multiple units, there will be a growing consensus for a standardized solution to solving them. This becomes the hospital's own unique best practice, developed by the very people who implement it every day—the frontline staff and their managers.

As this becomes more pronounced, two different types of problems will begin to coalesce: (1) problems that arise from a lack of process or a broken process and (2) problems that arise from a lack of adherence to the process. This is of huge importance to managers and leaders because, historically,

---

* Chapter 9 focuses on how to leverage your daily management system to fundamentally change the hospital's approach to discharges and is a good example of how starting with a standard problem-solving approach can expand standardization throughout the hospital.

the default assumption is that problems arise because people make mistakes; therefore, the key to eliminating problems is to ensure that people never make mistakes. This has resulted in a drift toward punitive management with little improvement on quality.

Now, though, as the daily management system becomes a vehicle for creating and implementing best practices, management will have a much clearer view into why things go wrong and can either address process issues through daily problem-solving or people issues through corrective action. Because management can now correctly diagnose the cause of the problem, they have a much better shot at correcting it.

Standard work for leadership then becomes a tool to liberate and share creativity. Using the plan–do–study–act cycle for problem-solving is a standard way to rapidly and accurately *understand* the problem—the creativity needed to actually *solve* the problem is still required. A standard approach to managing discharges allows anyone to quickly understand the current barrier to discharge, but creativity is required to solve them. In both cases, standard work allows managers to spend more time solving problems without compromising their level of understanding. On the other hand, it actually enhances the understanding of the problem, ensuring that the solutions are reached faster and are correct more often.

In essence, good standard work for managers allows them to operate at the top of their abilities a greater percentage of the day.

Building your own best practice is a continuous process. Daily rounds are a good first step as they get everyone in the hospital on the same page. From there, other pieces can be developed and implemented. It is good practice to develop standards around common areas—places and times where managers naturally congregate—and then move into practices that managers enforce individually. A good general flow of best-practice development looks something like the following:

1. Implement hospital-wide leadership rounds on all units to standardize problem-solving
2. Develop a standardized bed huddle and safety meeting
3. Standardize discharge management
4. Standardize the unit-level shift change meeting
5. Standardize the discharge work list in supporting areas

This is, of course, but one path of many that a hospital can take, but it starts at a point where senior leaders have good visibility on the process and works outwards to where they have less visibility. This allows them to build the abilities of their management team collectively at first and individually later.

As this process unfolds, the day-to-day schedule of managers should become more and more prescriptive. The daily schedule of a unit manager may look something like the following:

- 8:00–8:30—Start of day huddle with charge nurse to review critical needs and discharge status of the unit
- 8:30–9:00—Address critical issues and prepare for leader rounds
- 9:00–9:30—Round with senior leader
- 9:30–10:00—Bed huddle and safety meeting
- 10:00–12:00—Work the prioritized discharges
- 12:00–13:00—Lunch
- 13:00–15:00—Manage personnel and critical issues
- 15:00–16:30—Meetings (as needed)
- 16:30–17:00—End-of-day huddle with charge nurse

At this point, you are likely thinking that such a schedule is untenable in the chaos of the hospital, and, currently, you are likely correct. The reason though is not that this is impossible but rather that we have not been trained to manage this way and we do not have the systems in place to facilitate its implementation.

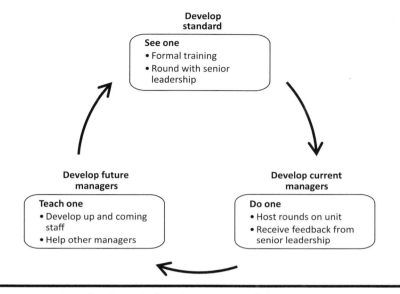

Figure 6.1   Standard work development cycle.

Fortunately, both are done incrementally, so, while the end result is currently impossible, the next step is not (Figure 6.1).

Developing Current Managers

Healthcare has a wonderful approach to learning technical skills that can be applied to process and leadership skills as well. The approach is as follows:

■ *See one*—see the skill being performed
■ *Do one*—perform the skill under supervision
■ *Teach one*—supervise another doing the skill

This approach is embodied in the model of the following:

■ Develop a standard
■ Develop current management
■ Develop future management

While we have covered the development of a standard in depth, the most salient point to remember is that it should be implemented one small change at a time. This is called *task loading* and is commonly used when teaching high-risk activities such as flying or scuba diving. The basic principle is to teach a task—such as how to taxi a plane or how to clear a mask—and slowly progress to more advanced skills as the basics are mastered.

This works in healthcare as well. Implement leadership rounds. Then, help the current cadre of managers learn how to use the rounds. Finally, help them develop people from their staff to use the rounds. Let everything settle and the new task become a habit before developing the next piece of standard work (Figure 6.2).

By starting with leader rounds, senior leadership give themselves the advantage of seeing not only every part of the hospital every day, but also every manager interacting with the standard every day. Senior leadership now has the daily opportunity to provide feedback to their managers. This is the do one phase of learning for managers.

For senior leaders, this is a time of coaching. Early on in the development of management standard work, this is also a time of accountability. Some managers will eagerly embrace

Task	Lean coach	Administration	Managers	Frontline staff
Morning rounds	Teach →	Do →	See	
		Teach ⇄	Do →	See
			Teach ⇄	(Do)
Bed huddle	Teach →	Do →	See	
		Teach ⇄	Do →	See
			Teach ⇄	(Do)
Hoshin planning	Teach →	Do →	See	
		Teach ⇄	Do →	See
			Teach ⇄	(Do)

Standard work created ⊐⊢

Figure 6.2   Learning cycle applied to standard work.

this new direction; some will actively oppose it; and the majority will remain undecided. The job of senior leadership is to establish the commitment level of the hospital. There is a delicate balance that must be struck between holding managers accountable to participation yet giving ample room for mistakes to be made as these mistakes are the bricks and mortar of learning.

The reality though is that many senior leaders will not be prepared to handle this degree of coaching. If the hospital has an expert resource, either internal or as a consultant, this person can help coach senior leaders as they themselves learn how to coach. While developing managers is critical to long-term success, this can only be done if senior leadership is able to develop their managers. Because the development of leadership skills has long been neglected in healthcare, *any* ability to coach is an unexpected and welcome benefit.

When an organization commits itself to something as deep and transformational as a Lean journey, it is committing itself to a paradigm shift. As Joel Parker points out in his *New Business of Paradigms* video, when the paradigm shifts, everyone goes back to zero. Thus, the leadership and management that are most accomplished under the old way of administration will become the most vulnerable under the new way because they have the most to unlearn.

Lean practitioners learn, begrudgingly, to embrace the *fuzzy middle* of a project—the vast expanse of uncertainty that links the identification of a problem to the solution that is finally reached. The same is true with managers and leaders, except that there is an additional twist that is thrown in.

> *The more capable a leader is, the more uncertainty they should feel when a new management system is in place.*

The reason this is true is that good leaders feel confident when leading into uncharted waters—they do not feel comfortable when leading differently into uncharted waters. What we are asking of them is to manage two facets of uncertainty. First, we are asking them to implement a drastically different management system. Second, we are asking them to implement it in a drastically different manner from something that they have ever implemented before. Thus, resistance from managers and senior leaders is, in equal parts, understandable and forgivable. The crux is for everyone to understand that everyone is on a learning curve and that mistakes are germane to the learning process. The role of your guide is to ensure that (a) mistakes are indeed made and (b) that they are leveraged into learning.

Developing managers first starts with developing senior leadership. This is not to say that current leadership is deficient any more than it would be to say that someone who has never before seen a body of water is deficient for not knowing how to kayak. It is rather to say though that learning and development must happen if the opposite shore is to be reached. So, it is paramount for senior leaders to recognize that it is okay to fail, even multiple times if necessary.

There is no ideal path to becoming a Lean organization or even becoming a Lean leader. The most successful Lean leaders are those who struggled the most early on yet remained equally humble and determined. There is no prize for becoming Lean quickly, only becoming Lean consistently. So, what then is a senior leader to do?

The first step is to enforce participation in the process. If a manager is missing once during rounds, that is likely due to factors that are out of his or her control. If he or she consistently misses rounds, then he or she is refusing to participate in the process. This is an accountability issue that must be addressed.

If the unit progresses in fits and starts along the cultural continuum, and occasionally regresses, this is progress, and the manager is attempting to bring the entire unit along. If the unit stalls early on and makes a forward movement, then the manager is likely refusing to participate in the process. Because standards can help leaders differentiate between problems with the process and problems with the people, this will become abundantly apparent as time progresses.* If a manager continuously refuses to participate, he or she needs discipline or replacement. If he or she continuously fails, he or she needs coaching and help.

Ultimately, like any true Lean initiative, the bedrock should be a genuine respect for people. Respect where they are coming from, what challenges they are dealing with, and what effort they are putting into the process, and respect them enough to expect their full commitment.

Because this is a three-step process, the learning for managers is not complete until they propagate their learning to those who will follow them. Developing the new cadre of managers is the ultimate and final step in building leader standard work.

Developing Future Managers

The first step in developing future managers is identifying those with management potential. Because this has historically been done based on clinical skills or intuition, there have been gaps in identifying management talent. With no standard on which to base these judgments, is it surprising that the current method of promotion is less than ideal?

As standard work for managers becomes more pervasive in its scope, the ability of the organization to identify and groom future leaders grows. This helps close a major gap in leadership development for many hospital systems.

In general, the large hospital systems have leadership development paths in place to help directors develop into

---

* The audit tool will remove much of the subjectivity when evaluating management.

executives and to help executives hone their abilities. What is lacking though is a path from the front line into management and director spots. Because there are so many employees, it is virtually impossible for these development paths to be centrally managed. However, management standard work allows these development paths to be locally managed in a standard way.

One of the main functions of a Lean management system is to push decision making down to the lowest level that is possible. This not only frees up both managers' and leaders' time to focus on more important issues, but also serves as a development process for future leaders. While staff empowerment is accepted as a good thing, it has proved incredibly difficult to actually implement. The reason is that there are no guide rails to facilitate this empowerment.

Lean Daily Management though provides that through specified daily activities. As your organization builds pieces of the management standard work, and implements them, it becomes a simple matter to teach staff how to perform to them. For instance, once your hospital develops a standard method for managing discharges, and managers learn how to run that method, the next and final step is to teach key informal leaders on the floor on how to run the discharge board. Because there are clearly defined actions that must take place, the manager, and even senior leadership, can quickly and accurately judge if the board runner is correctly managing the floor.

The end result is that managers now become coaches for their people, and a metric of their success is not how well they as a manager run the discharge board but rather how many of their people can run the board. Because discharges are now run visually and by the front line, the manager has more free time to problem-solve issues and improve the process.

This technique can be used for any of the standardized pieces that are developed for any level of leadership. When done correctly, this process of standardizing pieces of management into self-developed best practices leads to greater creativity and more freedom for managers. While this is at first counterintuitive, it makes sense when we understand that creativity and problem-solving are finite resources. As a manager's day wears on the more decisions that they are called to make, the more their ability to make good decisions degrades. Removing unnecessary decisions is a well-recognized solution to this problem and is a key point in a management system.*

The paradox of a daily management system is this: fewer decisions lead to greater control. This is a major stumbling block for many leaders during the implementation process. Historically, most organizations get stuck in command-and-control leadership structures. Because this concentrates decision making at the top of the leadership structure, it places an upper limit on how much information the organization can process, and thus how reactive it can be to changing circumstances. Because conditions change rapidly in hospitals, this centralization of decision making slows down the responsiveness of the house. For instance, floors are often unaware of spikes in the ED or L&D census leading to long waits in those areas. Intensive care units are unaware of the OR volume leading to patients being held in the postanesthesia care unit until step-down patients can be taken to the floor.

This lack of coordination so common to hospitals is a result of the bottleneck of leadership: one that can be broken with a solid daily management system. By providing a structure for both information flow and management practices, decision making can be done at much lower levels of the organization while at the same time providing a better view of the organization as a whole to senior leadership. With enough refinement, this information that is trickled up can even become predictive and anticipatory instead of historical and reactive.

---

* Steve Jobs famously removed wardrobe decisions from his plate with his trademark black t-shirt and jeans in an effort to save his brainpower for important decisions.

At the start though, the goal is to simply begin developing and hardwiring management best practices and then to train future managers on them. If this is a way to develop staff into managers, then the question becomes how to develop managers into leaders.

Converting Managers into Leaders

While the terms *management* and *leadership* have been used a bit interchangeably in this chapter, it is necessary to draw a line of distinction between them. For the purposes of this book, a simple-enough line is to think of management as the technical day-to-day activities of running a hospital. These are the things that can be codified, likely have best practices built around, and packaged into the daily management system. Leadership can be thought of as all of the soft skills that are so vital to handling the ambiguity of the hospital. Things such as people development, crisis management, strategic thinking, and advanced problem-solving all fit in to this bucket.

It is important to note that these two buckets are not confined to their own roles, that is, there is a great deal of leadership that is required of managers and a great deal of management that is required of senior leadership. So, while building and propagating best practices will develop the managerial abilities of people, another approach is needed to develop leadership abilities. The missing piece is a formalized mentoring structure that supports continuous development.

Continuous Development and Continuous Improvement

Continuous improvement and continuous development of the work force are inexorably linked (Figure 6.3). Staff cannot solve more complex problems without more advanced problem-solving abilities, and the only way to develop these

| Continuous process improvement | Continuous people improvement |

Figure 6.3   People and process improvement cycle.

abilities is through solving the ever-increasingly complex problems. This flies in the face of the generally accepted practice of sending people to classroom training with the expectation of competence at the end. The problem with this approach is that ability comes from not only seeing but also doing and teaching. At the end of training, only a third of the see one, do one, teach one learning cycle has been achieved.

The solution to this is stunningly simple—once a task has been taught, the next phase of learning is for the student to perform it under supervision and then finally to teach it to another. Simple does not equate to easy though, and implementing such a coaching system is a major challenge when developing a Lean Daily Management system. Support from a coach that has implemented this type of coaching structure, as well as a strong dose of patience, is highly recommended at this point.

A good starting point for building this structure is to follow the existing management hierarchy. A boss acts as the mentor for their employees. This structure has a couple of limiting factors though. First, the mentoring required may not be the boss's area of expertise. In the long term, this will be solved by letting employees have mentors throughout the organization or *cross-building* mentor-to-mentee relationships. This is too big a step though to start with.

The second limitation is that many hospital managers have very broad spans of control. It is not uncommon for some nursing floors or EDs to have more than 100 employees yet only one or two managers. This can be solved by *depth-building* mentor-to-mentee relationships. This depth building can begin on day 1 and slowly grow. The key is to identify the handful of employees that can function as future mentors to their peers.

Fortunately, identifying these employees is a straightforward process. See which ones naturally gravitate to the daily management system and try to make it their own. As they do, they will naturally hit roadblocks that require assistance from management. This is the perfect opportunity for managers to slide into the mentor role. If the hospital has hired a Lean coach to help with the deployment of the daily management system, he or she will provide invaluable guidance at this stage.

As the new daily management system gains traction, more and more employees will become involved. The manager at this point will have *super users* who understand how the mechanics work, have mastered the fundamentals of problem-solving, and can act as mentors for the employees who are just beginning to show interest.

This approach underscores a very important point for all leaders to bear in mind during the rollout of their Lean Daily Management system. Do not worry about the managers and employees who do not quickly embrace the change. There is a natural tendency to win over everyone before making progress and even to focus on the *most critical* naysayer the way we would naturally focus on the most critical patient. This is a mistake because once they have been convinced to come along, the other employees have languished, and the entire program bogs down.

Instead, focus on the most enthusiastic people first. Not only is this much more easy (and fun), but also it ensures that their enthusiasm meets with quick success instead of stagnation and failure. Ultimately, it will be their enthusiasm and achievement that will bring the more reluctant into the fold. This is a huge relief to managers because your success is not dictated by how poorly your least engaged employee is performing in the system, but rather how far your most enthusiastic ones are pushing it forward.

Mentoring employees may seem like an ambiguous and daunting challenge. The key is to start simple and structured. The *A3* can be utilized to aid with this. In typical Lean projects, A3s are used to manage the project. While there are a plethora of different formats, most A3s generally have the following structure:

- Problem definition
- Current state analysis
- Future state
- Implementation of tasks
- Future state verification

The trick to a successful A3 template is to keep it as simple as possible. While it is customary to use one side of an 11-×-17-inch sheet of paper, this is not at all necessary. (A3 is the paper size for the metric equivalent of an 11-×-17-inch sheet.) Two regular-sized sheets of paper with the form printed on them, stapled together, are perfectly fine (Figure 6.4).*

The value of using the A3 is twofold. First, it forces simplicity. Anything too complicated to fit on the A3 needs to be simplified down so that it is easily understood. This simplicity also makes the A3 process approachable. While putting together a slide deck for a presentation is complex and potentially scary for a frontline employee, simply writing down the current progress by hand and sitting down with the manager for 5–10 minutes for feedback is easy.

Second, it forces transparency. Because the A3 is both visual and comprehensive, it is easy to see where in the problem-solving process your employee is currently struggling.

---

* You can download A3 templates and instructions from LeanDailyManagement .com/downloads.

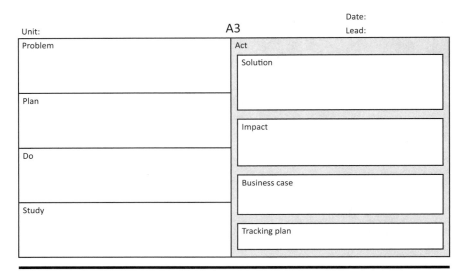

Figure 6.4   A3 example.

This allows for clear and continuous feedback that keeps the entire project from becoming stuck.

While A3s are most often used as project management tools in the context of the daily management system, they are also used as coaching tools. This requires a different mindset from mentors. Here, the goal is not to solve the problem but rather to develop the employee through the solving of the problem. This will be very difficult for managers initially because it requires you to let your people struggle through the problem until they solve it. Your job is not to suggest solutions but rather to ask clarifying questions and point out weaknesses in their thinking.

While this may seem like a painfully slow way to improve the organization, it is actually blisteringly fast. Done correctly, the result of this patience is a work force that not only can detect, measure, diagnose, and solve seemingly intractable problems, but also is eager to do so. The power of this competitive advantage cannot be underestimated because it cannot be easily duplicated. It is possible to move the organization from measuring employee engagement once a year to actively engaging employees every day.

Most hospitals have some sort of employee suggestion system. Most of those that do either do not actively run that system or, if they do, do so poorly. This includes your competitors. If your hospital is able to not only tap into the ideas of its people but also to give them the skills, mentoring, and freedom to proactively and scientifically implement ideas and solve problems, you will be able to become incomparably more nimble to the market and more responsive to your patients. While your competition is focused on delivering a financial result next quarter, you will have built a deeply embedded edge that will continue to not only deliver results but also improve its ability to deliver results, not just next quarter but for years to come.

This strikes at the heart of what it really means to become a Lean organization. It is not about doing more with less, or cutting waste, or even improving quality. It is really about tapping into each employee, investing in them, developing them, and then empowering them in a structured manner. Not only does this result in lower costs and higher quality, but also, and more importantly, resolves into more meaning for your people. This becomes a system for respecting people. Healthcare is filled with the most compassionate, highly trained people of any industry. All that is needed is a management system that can unleash their potential.

Once your people are working the new daily management system, they will naturally begin to ask, "What is the next step?" While much has been written on how to set goals for an organization and bring alignment to the day-to-day operations, the focus has largely been on how to start at the top of the organization and push the direction down. At this point though, your staff will start reaching up looking for that direction, and, when they do, your hospital will need to be ready.

Chapter 7

Establishing Direction

Diversity in counsel, unity in command.

Cyrus the Great

Introduction

Once daily rounding is well established and problem-solving becomes more complex and cross-departmental with regular use of A3s, the natural tendency for leadership is to sit back and let the program hum along. There is nothing inherently wrong with doing precisely that for a while. In fact, if the whole of the hospital achievement is to simply arrive at that point, that should be considered a huge win, and it will pay dividends for years to come. However, there is much more that can be accomplished.

As teams begin to work with other departments in a systematic way, they will begin to encounter the division of interests that naturally occurs in hospitals. For instance, pre-op, the OR and PACU may streamline patient flow through the OR and cut the turnover time, yet, in the process, inconvenience physicians. Dietary Unit may develop a way to deliver food to rooms in under 20 minutes that requires additional help from an already stretched nursing staff. Clinics and the ED often have competing aims. Which patients are admitted first to crowded floors—ED, OR, or transfers—is often a battle of trade-offs. The core problem is that there is not a shared set of operational values, which leads to competing goals and zero-sum gain thinking.

These values are different from the typical set of values that most organizations use. Values such as *trust, accountability, compassion,* and *integrity* are little more than meaningless platitudes and offer no direction to staff and managers trying to improve their processes. In fact, values such as these can be universally accepted by everyone in the organization, and these operational conflicts will continue unabated. They may even be intensified.

Consider the conflict among the prioritization of patient admission. There is often deep-seated frustration between the OR and the ED on this issue because each group is advocating for their patients. The charge for the nurses in each group to be compassionate leads them to value their patients' experiences above all the other patients in the hospital because they experience their discomfort firsthand. This is not a bad thing at all. Nurses are supposed to advocate for their patients. The problem is that there is no agreed-upon value. As a result, the solution presented by one group often comes at the expense of another.

What is missing are a set of operational values: ideal goals that are true in every situation that can act as a beacon for the direction that a better solution lies. This type of thinking is already replete in the medical world. A good example is the concept that no one should ever do harm to a patient. This shared value cuts across roles and departments. It is an ideal that is rarely, if ever, completely achieved, yet it acts as an ideal that should continuously be strived for. It leads to questions such as the following:

1. What is the least invasive treatment option?
2. How can we make the patient feel as comfortable as possible without compromising care?

3. There is no skilled nursing facility that can take this patient at the moment—what are the best alternatives that are available?

Note that this value—do no harm—does not answer questions but rather acts as a guide to asking questions when confronted with a problem. In the same way, there needs to be an operational set of values that will generate the right questions as people struggle to resolve operational problems. We call these values *True North*.

True North

True North is a set of shared operational values that every department can use when developing solutions. They should be few in number, light in complexity, and useful in application. Here are some sample True North values that hospitals have used:

■ Patients never wait.
■ Nurses and physicians always have what they need, when they need it, where they need it.
■ Discharges happen before noon.
■ Every patient has a room when and where they need it.

These values are unattainable. At some point, patients will wait on something. Nurses will never have absolutely everything that they need all of the time. Discharges will inevitably happen late in the day. When the floors are full, stretchers will inevitably line some hallways. The fact that these are unattainable is fine though because these are not goals but rather ideals.

The typical approach by traditional management is to craft these ideals into goals as expressed by a percentage. For instance, a common goal that many managers are held to is a certain percentage of patients who are discharged before noon. While this is not inherently bad, it is also not pervasive. Whereas the floor manager may be held to that goal, the laboratory and radiology managers may not be, yet they may be major drivers of late discharges. Instead, their goal may be to take care of urgent orders first. Thus, patients awaiting discharges are a lower priority for them.

Managers may compensate for this by having the hospitalist put in his or her orders as stat orders. This bumps other orders from elsewhere in the hospital until they too abuse the stat flag. As a result, the bulk of orders are now stat orders, diluting the impact of a stat order. Whereas the departments and units may change, this storyline is often repeated.

A well-crafted set of True North values can help navigate this morass by pointing toward what a successful solution should look like. No longer is it acceptable to simply reduce discharges after noon to under 25%. Instead, a solution must be found to reduce discharges by some amount without violating any of the other True North values anywhere else in the hospital. The question shifts from "How can we achieve 75% discharge before noon?" to "How can we get one more patient out the door before noon, consistently, without causing delays elsewhere?" The shift is subtle yet powerful as it requires holistic thinking beyond the immediate impact.

This, in turn, requires a different question from leadership. The question to the manager before was, "Why is your discharge number before noon so low?" Now, it is, "What steps did you take this month to improve flow?" The focus shifts from goal achievement to incremental progress that is supported by the daily rounding system.

One major objection to the True North values is that they are not linked to financial metrics. After all, eliminating wait time for patients is all well and good, but what is the financial reward for doing so? A well-built strategy map and a balanced scorecard can help bridge the gap between the operational metric and the financial impact.

Balanced Scorecards and Strategy Maps

Strategy maps, developed by Robert Kaplan and David Norton, are a good way of visualizing the drivers of financial impact. They are designed to work in conjunction with an organization's balanced scorecard by showing the relationships among the sections of the scorecard. Because balanced scorecards are already in wide use by hospitals, they serve as a useful hub for strategy. Before diving into their use, a brief primer on the scorecard is in order.

Historically, for-profit organizations are rated solely on their financial performance. Solvency, profitability, capitalization rates, debt/asset ratios, income/expense ratios, and other ways of looking at a company's holdings and cash flow are the standard tools for evaluating the investment potential and thus the effectiveness of management. This approach has several limitations.

First, this approach does a poor job of evaluating the success of a nonprofit organization. The goal of a for-profit organization is to retain as much profit from its customer base as possible, whereas the goal of a nonprofit organization is to disburse as much money as possible to its customer base. Thus, simply measuring profit and profitability is essentially meaningless for nonprofit organizations.

Second, financial indicators are lagging indicators. They show what the organization has done. The prevailing belief is that, with enough history, an organization develops a trend that can be used to forecast the future. While trending and forecasting are a valuable exercise, as every investment prospectus states, "Past performance is no guarantee of future results."

Third, financial indicators can indicate that there is trouble in the organization and can sometimes even identify where the issue lies (though this is often simply where the problem manifests, not originates). These indicators though are deplorable at identifying why trouble is happening or what can be done to solve it. Leaders are left with few options such as across-the-board cuts or layoffs. Too often though, these cuts and layoffs go too deep and are too indiscriminate resulting in future budget increases and hiring binges.

The balanced scorecard is an attempt to cut through these limitations by balancing how the organization is measured (Figure 7.1). Other metrics, such as operational metrics, customer metrics, employee metrics, and quality metrics, are included to *balance out* the weight of the financial metrics. These other metrics can show impact beyond financial results, reveal the leading indicators for financial indicators, and help pinpoint opportunities for improvement (the subject of Chapter 8).

This sample scorecard would work reasonably well in a typical hospital. However, as the saying goes, "If you have been in one hospital, you have been in one hospital," so modification will be needed. This should serve as a decent starting point though.

While this scorecard shows a broader range of objectives, the linkage among them is not immediately clear. A strategy map of the scorecard will help cut through this ambiguity to reveal the linkage (Figure 7.2).

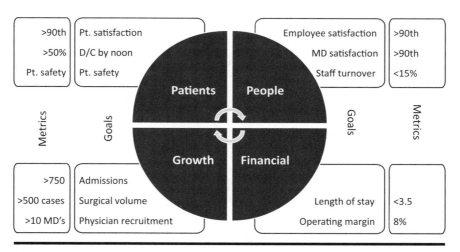

Figure 7.1 Balanced scorecard. D/C, discharge.

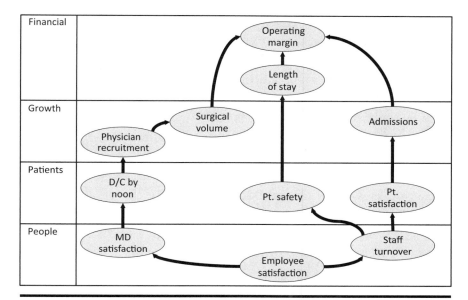

Figure 7.2   Strategy map.

The relationships in this map are directional only, not quantifiable. For instance, if employee engagement is increased by 10%, how much will patient safety increase? These data are not readily available and, due to the complex nature of hospital operations, cannot be substituted with industry averages. All this map does is to formalize a recognition that improving a driver will have a positive impact on the derivative. Improving employee engagement will increase patient safety.

While this is a bit of an organizational leap of faith, it does have a practical purpose. It provides a starting point for problem-solving. If patient safety is a concern, leaders can look at the drivers of that based on the strategy map to help identify how and where to solve the problem. If a driver of patient safety is also a concern, then that becomes a point to start investigating.

It may be, though, that there are no drivers on the map that are out of line, yet a problem still exists. This means one of two things: (1) either a driver is not on the map (or one that is there is not properly captured) or (2) the issue has no driver, and the root cause of the problem exists at that level of the map. Either way, the discussion is now focused on one of the two possibilities.

A good strategy map will help visually tie several areas of concern into a single problem. Poor financial performance may be a result of high readmissions (a patient safety measure) that are, in turn, linked to a poor discharge process and low employee satisfaction. Instead of treating each of these as individual problems as is typical, where the chief financial officer tackles the financial issue, the quality director focuses on the readmissions, the case manager handles the discharge problem, and the human resources works to improve nursing satisfaction, a true cross-functional team can be assembled to work on the entire problem.

The key to making this work though is understanding when something is out of line. Fortunately, this is fairly simple to do, at least initially. By developing a balanced scorecard that conforms to industry standards,* you can then benchmark against the industry averages to create a starting assessment of your hospital. Soon though, if the hospital has not already done so, you will be ready to develop your own metrics or *key performance indicators* (KPIs).

Developing Hospital KPIs

The use of KPIs is fairly standard among the larger hospital systems, as are balanced scorecards. If your organization already uses these tools, the remainder of this chapter will be familiar. However, before an organization can begin to cascade strategy down through the organization, a solid understanding

---

* Like everything else in this book, free examples and templates of balanced scorecards and strategy maps can be found at www.LeanDailyManagement.com that you can customize and use in your hospital.

of KPIs and how they differ from the metrics on the daily rounding boards is needed.

KPIs are aggregate numbers, usually expressed in a percentage, that offer a high-level view of how the organization is performing in specific areas. They can be used at the hospital level: lower at a department level or higher at a corporate level. Because they are aggregate, they represent historic data, usually from the previous month. While they do an excellent job of gauging where the hospital is, they are not very useful as problem-solving tools.

By contrast, the metrics on the boards are specific fallouts—never expressed as a percentage and poor indicators of performance—yet highly useful for problem-solving. Because the focus is on simplicity and ease of use, they are captured with a hash mark when the fallout happens. The focus of problem-solving is understanding the root cause; therefore, the metrics are never aggregated into a percent as this would be wasted effort. Naturally, much data are missed when collected in this manner; thus, the metrics are not a good indication of how well the process is working. This is best left to KPIs.

Because metrics and KPIs function differently, one that is focused on problem-solving and the other that is concentrated on reporting, they can be used together for integrated improvement. Often, KPIs do not function well as metrics. For instance, they may be expressed in terms of percentage or average and need to be converted into specific fallouts. Usually, this conversion is fairly direct. For instance, if there is a goal of average ED turnaround time of 180 minutes, the fallout could start out as any patient in the ED who stays longer than 180 minutes. However, this will generate too many fallouts to track effectively as a metric. If, for instance, there are 100 visits to the ED per day, logic indicates that half of them will take longer than the average, and the other half will take shorter than the average. Thus, if the average time is 180 minutes, then staff will be collecting data on 50 patients per day. If the target average is 180 minutes but the actual average is higher, the number of patients greater than 180 minutes will increase well beyond 50 per day (Figure 7.3).

Instead, a quick look at the data will help determine an appropriate metric. Creating a quick histogram or bell curve of the data will show the frequency that different wait times occur. In this example, a good target metric is the ED turn-around time that is greater than 240 minutes because it limits the data collection to a manageable number. In this case, we can expect 10 fallouts per day.

This is counterintuitive for many managers and administrators because the natural assumption is that holding the metric to 180 minutes will cause a greater urgency to hit the targeted KPI. This assumption comes from a fundamental misunderstanding of how to improve operations. If the problem was simply that staff were not working hard or fast enough, then this could be a legitimate strategy. Yet, this is exceedingly rare in the hospital setting. Instead, the goal is to find the process problems that are leading to the wait times. By scoping the problem area to the most extreme cases, we give ourselves two advantages.

First, we reduce the daily workload of collecting data. This is especially important in patient care areas. Any time running the management system interferes with patient care, something needs to give, and it is never patient care. Keeping the data light helps prevent this from occurring.

Second, by focusing on the more extreme fallouts, we can move the metric the most with the least amount of effort

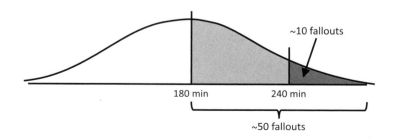

Figure 7.3 Metric selection bell curve.

because we are addressing the fallouts that impact the average the most. This is not an ironclad rule though, and thought should be given before blindly following this path. It very well may be that a common process problem that delays every patient is occurring, giving the opportunity for a large shift in the KPI with relatively little effort. This can be captured though even when focusing on the more extreme fallouts by looking for any source of delay. Looking for the 4 activity wastes can help identify these sources of delay.

Another reason the KPIs often make poor metrics is that they do not cover something that an area has real control of. This concept is expanded in Chapter 8 as it relates to strategy, but, in essence, many KPIs are outcomes that cannot be directly influenced. The ED turnaround time, for instance, cannot be directly managed because it is the result of many subprocesses involving many different actors. Thus, it is not a simple matter to improve these KPIs. Fortunately, the boards naturally break down these KPIs into metrics that can be controlled through the rigorous application of the plan–do–study–act process. As the problem-solving cycles continue, they will dig down into the primary drivers of the KPI problems and root them out. As always, when faced with this, trust your staff and the process.

At this point in the process, your boards are up; rounds are occurring; and staff are engaged, empowered, and aligned with each other. Problems are systematically being rooted out and solved. The departments are working together on issues that cross functional boundaries. If you have made it this far, congratulations are in order. (If not, do not worry; this takes a lot of work and a long time—patience and consistency are key.) Many Lean efforts stall long before this point as leadership changes or gets distracted by the next crisis or the next promise of easy solutions to complex problems. If you and the team have arrived here, then you may count yourself among the elite of Lean management teams. There is one more step, one final gearshift, before your Lean Daily Management system can truly operate at peak performance. Your hospital should be ready to develop a long-term strategy and cascade that strategy down to the front line so that, every day, every department will be able to answer whether they are winning or losing in achieving the strategic goals of the hospital.

Chapter 8

Cascading Strategy

I have always found that plans are useless, but planning is indispensable.

Dwight D. Eisenhower

Introduction

There is a gap between strategy development and strategy execution. In many organizations, this gap is large enough to relegate the developed strategy to irrelevance—yet another dusty binder with little use other than evaluating the year once it is over. The spread of strategic ability among hospitals is very wide—some are quite adept at it, and some do not even do strategy, whereas most lie somewhere in between. This chapter will start from the ground up and move quickly to the more advanced ways to use Lean Daily Management to support and drive strategic development and deployment. As such, the weak areas typically encountered in hospital strategies may or may not apply to your organization.

There is an unwritten belief that strategy execution is a given and that failure to execute the organization's strategy is a failure of enforcement. The result is that leaders find themselves driving metrics down and using them as a scale in which to hold their managers accountable.

The first side effect of this approach is that the *why* is lost in the process. By the time the organizational goal reaches the frontline staff, its linkage to the overall health of the organization and the long-term vision is often murky. Without the why, the impetus for compliance becomes "because I said so." Engagement drops, and the opportunity for frontline staff to identify other better ways of achieving the objective is lost.

The second side effect is that managing the strategy becomes impossible. Because the strategic metrics are pushed through the levels of the organization rather than developed through them, the link between daily activity and strategic output is not established. Without understanding how long-term strategy is achieved at a daily level, how can leaders know if they are winning or losing on any given day?

Reliance on monthly data delays the detection of issues and hides the causes of these issues. Just as in the early phases of the development of the daily management system, the focus was on daily problem-solving, now, the focus becomes daily strategic alignment. This can be done through a process that is known as *hoshin kanri*.

Hoshin Kanri

Hoshin kanri (also known as *hoshin*) is an iterative, interactive approach to strategy creation, deployment, and execution. The term loosely translates to *direction management*, showing an emphasis on managing the organization toward the strategic goal. This stands in contrast to the *fire-and-forget* mentality behind so much of the way that organizations currently drive strategy.

Part of the problem is that, like *quality*, *strategy* is ill defined and nebulous. There is a general concept of what strategy is but no operational definition. Just as quality is often defined as synonymous with *good*, leaving a meaningless term that cannot be used to drive action, strategy is defined simply as a plan of action. Strategy is synonymous with the strategic plan. However, there are limitations to this definition.

First, the planning phase happens once and is deployed over the course of the year. Whereas the plan is static, the environment is fluid and responsive meaning that the moment that the strategic planning session is done, the plan starts to become obsolete. Like months-long improvement projects that get mired in the data collection and analysis phases by the time that the actual improvement takes place, the situation has morphed. The solution to the disconnect between the planning and the action in both a process improvement project and strategic planning is the same—implement small things quickly and do so continuously. We will cover how to do this in depth later in this chapter.

The second limitation to traditional strategic planning is a lack of how to accomplish the steps. Strategic plans contain a multitude of assumptions that may or may not be true. For instance, if a major goal of the hospital is to increase the OR volume by 15% over the next three years, the question becomes "how?" The traditional approach is to find the weak spots in the OR by benchmarking metrics, with the idea that returning these metrics to be in line with comparable hospitals will solve the problem.

Yet, this still does not explain how the strategy will be executed. Part of this is the inability of managers to improve metrics. Because administration is so far removed from the day-to-day activities, they are naturally unaware of how to solve them. This is not a problem of capability but rather of proximity. The administration simply are not close enough to know the gritty details well enough to actually solving the problem. Thus, the weight of improvement falls to the manager with the assumption being that if a manager fails to meet his or her goals, a new manager is needed. At this point, where strategy and process improvement converge, a system is needed.

The second part of the difficulty behind executing strategy is that certain goals may not even be attainable, or, if they are, they may be economically unfeasible. The physical structure of the hospital drives much of the waste that hampers performance. This impact is not visible at the strategic planning level yet deeply affects the feasibility of the strategic goals. Often, this problem will not reveal itself until long after the planning session is done, and key metrics have failed to move far enough to support the strategy.

Finally, strategic plans put full focus on the goals yet do not pay attention to the behaviors that drive the results to achieve those goals. A goal is, by definition, an external result that cannot be directly achieved. For instance, if your goal is to lose 10 pounds in six months, you have a goal that you cannot directly control. Yet, you can measure progress each month by stepping on the scale and charting progress. The scale will tell you *where* you are in your weight loss journey, but it will not tell you *why* you are there or *what* the next step is. Because of that, dieters who only focus on the goal of losing weight will fail to meet their goal.

The paradox is that, to attain a goal, you first have to stop paying attention to the goal and instead pay attention to the behaviors that will achieve the goal. So, to successfully lose weight, daily weigh-ins are insufficient. If, though, the focus becomes the daily habit of eating the right food at the right amount combined with a set amount of exercise, the weight loss happens on its own.

Of course, all of these variables (and many more) need to be quantified and tracked daily. These are the behaviors that will achieve the goal of weight loss. Notice that when this perspective shifts, no longer are you tracking daily or monthly your progress to the goal, but rather you are tracking daily your achievement of your objectives. You can answer, with certainty, whether or not you are winning or losing the achievement of your goal on any given day. More importantly, if you are not, you can clearly identify what went wrong and why and correct that behavior the next day.

This same type of thinking can be used to drive the strategic plan throughout the hospital. Think of the strategic goals as the amount of weight loss that is desired from the previous example. Like weight loss, merely focusing on those goals, even if done daily, will not result in their achievement. This is because, even if measured daily, you cannot answer whether the hospital is winning or losing on any given day in its strategy execution. For instance, if the goal is volume through the ED, simply tracking it will not tell you why the volume is what it is. Did something change in the hospital to result in the spike or dip? Is there an external factor that is changing the landscape? Is it simply natural variation and not the result of any larger trend? Because these questions cannot be answered, true progress to the goal cannot be measured.

Like eating and exercise behaviors that can be directly managed to influence weight loss, which cannot be directly managed, the behaviors that can influence patient volume need to be identified, quantified, and developed into metrics. While standard ED metrics are often a good place to start, deeper metrics may be needed. Wait times are often a standard measure. The problem though is who controls wait times? Wait times themselves are smaller goals, not behaviors. Thus, they cannot be directly managed.

This is where the hard work of digging into the drivers of these goals begins. Like someone who is beginning his or her weight loss journey, the hospital can benefit tremendously from a coach who can identify and quantify key behaviors and turn them into a metric that can be managed daily, if not more frequently. The dieter learns to improve his or her physical weight by controlling his or her daily habits, and the hospital learns to improve their patient wait by managing their daily habits.

Successful implementation of a strategic plan requires pulling the vision back in time from the future to the present and pushing it down through the layers of management to the front line. These two activities are distinctly different. Pulling a multiyear vision backwards involves laying out the timeline to achieve that vision by establishing milestones. The vision is narrowed down into manageable chunks of time.

Pushing the strategy down narrows the vision by scope. Units, then, break the vision down into what impact they can have individually. They can then craft their own strategic plan to achieve that piece of the vision.

The obvious problem with these approaches is that establishing the timeline does not change action on the front line, and every unit charting their own path to achieve the vision sacrifices cohesion among the units. The answer, equally obvious to see and difficult to do, is to establish the strategic implementation timeline and then cascade that timeline down to the front line.

The problem typically encountered is that while cohesion is maintained, traction is lost as the strategic plan becomes increasingly irrelevant as it trickles down.

Catchball

The answer is to leverage the why and where of senior leadership and management with the how of frontline staff. Provided that you have invested the time to properly build your management system and the engagement and buy-in of your staff, the infrastructure is already in place. In fact, the whole point of building the management system has been this from the beginning. All that needs to be mastered now is the art of the cascade. An approach known as *catchball* can be used for this. In fact, you are likely already using this approach to develop your strategic timeline. Now, you can use it to push out strategy to the hospital floor as well.

Think about the last strategy session that the hospital had. Most likely, there was a lot of discussion about what the long-term vision of the hospital should be. This discussion can be thought of as a session of catchball. The chief executive officer (CEO) tosses out a vision for the future. Senior leadership discusses it, modifies it, and tosses it back. The CEO considers their input and then tosses their input back. This process continues until a consensus is reached about what the vision needs to be (Figure 8.1).

This process is long and involved, but, at the end, there is a strong, simple vision that the entire leadership team understands. The typical action at this point is to build a timeline and start driving the organization toward the future. From the leadership's perspective, there is a clear path that must be traversed. Consider though the perspective of middle management and frontline staff. Because they were not involved in the process of generating the plan, they have very little ownership of its achievement. This buy-in can happen through a few more games of catch.

Once the strategic timeline for the organization is established, the catchball sessions shift vertically. Senior leaders now play catch with their direct reports. The big difference here is that the communication is two directional. Leaders are

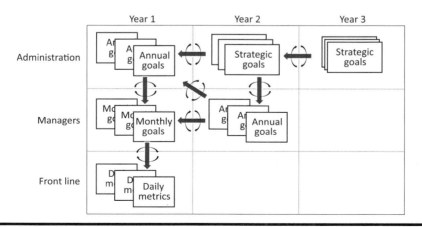

Figure 8.1   Catchball diagram.

looking for feedback rather than compliance. Done well, the goal should change with input from middle management. In some cases, it will need to be relaxed, in others, tightened, and in some cases, the goal itself will need to be reworked.

Of course, to do this right, managers will need to solicit the input of their staff. The catchball game shifts to the front line. The manager, the CEO of his or her own area, conducts a strategic session with his or her *company* (the unit) to establish their own timeline to achieve the goal that is set for them. Many times, this will reveal that the goal is the wrong goal, or poorly defined or scoped, or incorrectly measured. The next step of catchball is to work its way back up to the senior leader.

Catchball is supposed to be a messy, continuous process. It violently breaks the neat, clean box where strategy currently resides. The usual approach of planning the year beforehand, executing that plan, and repeating the cycle the following year is replaced by constant establishing of, tweaking of, deviation from, and correcting toward the strategic plan. The sterile, dead strategic plan is now alive, both driving the hospital and changed by it.

PRODUCTION

He who will not economize will have to agonize.

Confucius

Once you have your management system up and running, with good commitment from leadership, engagement from the staff, and progress on the part of your managers, your hospital is now ready to take the next step. There is much more to Lean Daily Management than simply walking around every morning and checking in on units to evaluate their current progress on independent problem-solving. Now, it is time to start really driving the system to deliver hard, tangible results that are sustainable.

Before moving on to this step though, it is worth pausing to evaluate where your hospital is. Are all of the necessary components in place? Here are some questions to ask to help you determine if it is time yet:

1. Are all routes walked every day, without exception, by senior leadership?
2. Are staff properly using the plan–do–study–act cycle to problem-solve?
3. Are managers empowering their staff, or are they stuck in command and control?
4. Are managers holding their staff accountable to the board?
5. Are the staff ready for the next challenge?
6. Is everyone embracing red?

The answers to these questions will undoubtedly vary tremendously by the area of the hospital. This is completely normal. All you need is to discover areas that are indeed ready to bring the whole system together. Invest in these areas first, and allow the others to progress naturally.

Your management system is designed to cut across many units in a uniform manner that allows some of the deep, intractable operational problems to be tackled in an organized fashion by everyone who is involved. You are now ready to harness the creative power of your work force and channel it in a constructive manner.

There are several problems that all hospitals seem to struggle with. These problems are cross-functional, yet, to date, most hospitals have taken a siloed approach to solving them. This is understandable, as traditional hospital management is structured around siloes and cost centers with little thought to upstream and downstream effects or spillover costs. This fractured approach makes truly seeing and understanding the problem difficult.

Your Lean Daily Management system though can aggregate all of the disparate data and show you where the errors are happening and, more importantly, why, on a daily basis. At this point though, your hospital is ready to move beyond only solving problems. It must learn to manage key processes in real time. Up to this point, you should have built leader discipline and daily rounding. You are now ready to implement visual controls and the supporting leader standard work that is necessary to support them.

The approaches to the following problems are not prescriptive. Because each hospital is unique, these should be viewed as suggested starting points for designing your own solutions. The commonality though is that any approach should leverage the daily rounding, incorporate the front line, and enable managers to quickly and easily make real-time decisions to affect the process before errors are made.

Chapter 9

Discharge Process

What is not started today is never finished tomorrow.

Johann Wolfgang von Goethe

Introduction

Patient flow is a major driver of costs. Patients who stay longer than necessary continue to consume valuable resources, not the least of which is a bed. Often, bed availability is the primary driver for long wait times in the ED and the OR. Because the last day is usually not paid for, every penny spent on patients who should have gone home hours earlier is a direct blow to the bottom line.

Understanding the hospital flow is critical to managing that flow. The typical Lean approach to do this is to use a value stream map (VSM) to map out the path of an average patient along with the time that is spent at each unit or area. This approach is limited though because hospitals have many types of patients, all flowing through different units. Thus, it becomes very difficult to show this graphically with a VSM.

Instead, a flow map can be used to show every unit, the flow of patients among them, and the unit length of stays and bed request delays (Figure 9.1). On this simple flow map, only the delay times and the unit length of stay are shown. Additional data such as volume, the number of discharges per day, or key discharge metrics can be overlaid as well.

This map is from a small hospital. Larger hospitals will have more complex maps with more intricate flows. In either case, the key is to find the system bottlenecks. In this hospital, like most others, there is a constraint at discharge. This is seen by the long discharge order that is written to the discharge times that are shown between the units and the discharge hexagon. Because improving discharges for every unit may be a larger challenge than can quickly be achieved, we can see from the map that the next greatest constraint is med/surg beds as those two units have the greatest bed request to patient movement times. Thus, by improving discharges on those two

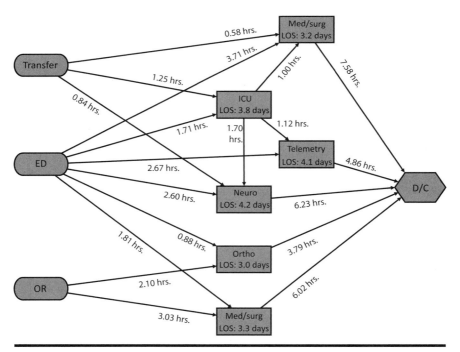

Figure 9.1   Patient flow map.

units, their ability to intake patients from the OR and the ED is enhanced.

Understanding the Problem

Patient flow is a major driver of costs. Patients who stay longer than necessary continue to consume valuable resources, not the least of which is a bed. Often, bed availability is the primary driver for long wait times in the ED. Because the last day is usually not billable, every penny spent on patients who should have gone home hours earlier is a direct blow to the bottom line.

Moving discharge times earlier in the day is a goal that is often met with a deep sense of futility. The common reasons given that patients cannot be discharged earlier are as follows:

- No rides are available because the family does not get off work until 5 p.m.
- Lack of reliable transportation.
- Physicians round late in the day.
- There is no place to disposition the patient.
- Mothers and babies are discharged separately at different times.
- Nursing staff are too busy to discharge in the morning.

As a result, hospitals seem to circle around the same cluster of solutions:

- Build a discharge lounge
- Issue cab vouchers
- Force physicians to write discharge orders by 9 a.m.
- Allow new mothers to board in room and do not include their discharge time in the numbers
- Hire discharge nurses to handle discharges

These solutions are hotly debated and, when implemented, never seem to actually improve discharge times. This is not surprising as objective data are rarely used when making these decisions. Because disagreement on a solution indicates a lack of understanding of the problem, the correct approach is to first study the problem and gain a solid understanding of what is happening and why. Fortunately, you now have a system in place that is designed to do precisely that.

The core problem in this case is almost always a failure to manage the discharge process. This can be easily confirmed by simply asking anyone on the floor, including the floor manager or case manager, how many discharges are expected for tomorrow. If they cannot answer with certainty, then that means that no one is managing the discharge process. If, as it is widely said, that discharge starts upon admission, then why is it that no one seems to know what tomorrow's discharge picture looks like?

If the core problem is a lack of management, then the solution is to hardwire a way to easily manage the discharge process. This solution needs to be all of the following:

■ Real time
■ Visual
■ Accountable
■ Standardized

Why are all four of them needed? If discharges are not managed in real time, then costly delays will creep into the process. The process must be made visual so that anyone at any time can easily see if he or she is falling behind. The people in the process must be held accountable to work with the management system, or else it will fail due to bad data. Finally, it must be standardized so that anyone can step in and operate the discharge process.

Developing a Solution

Hospitals have implemented these principles into their discharge management with marked success. They make the system real time by creating a board with the current status of every patient in every room. The data are visual because the only barriers to a timely discharge are called out making the entire discharge process easy to see. The process is accountable because everyday senior leadership audits the board during morning rounds. Furthermore, the process is standardized because all units measure the same data the same way and then flow that data to the central administration board daily.

The first step is to organize the discharging units to measure their defects the same way. The most common metric chosen is the *discharge after 12*, with a defect being any discharge that happens after 12 noon. It is critical that all units have the same target time and definition of a defect.

Once that is set, the next step is to generate the Pareto categories. While it is normally advisable to let the data naturally identify the categories, in this case, it is necessary to predetermine them for consistency. Here, the Pareto categories are simply the functional areas that are involved in the discharge process. The typical areas are as follows:

- ▪ Nursing
- ▪ Physicians
- ▪ Case management
- ▪ Radiology
- ▪ Laboratory
- ▪ Pharmacy
- ▪ Patient

Once the categories are defined, a discharge board can be built. This design is based on assembly boards that are used in manufacturing environments and will help the various groups both problem-solve and coordinate efforts around patient flow (Table 9.1).

The board is managed by the following rules:

- Every patient on the floor has an expected day of discharge that is updated by case management.
- Every patient is identified as either a possible discharge (D/C) by noon or a likely afternoon D/C.
- Barriers by role are written when identified and erased when solved.
- Every patient identified as a late discharge must have a barrier that is identified; patients as early discharge may have a barrier that is identified.
- When patients are discharged, they are erased from the board.
- At noon, any patients not discharged populate the run chart on the problem-solving board, and the barriers populate the Pareto chart.

Table 9.1   Discharge Board

Room	101	102	103	104
	Monday	Wednesday	Tuesday	Monday
Discharge (D/C) by noon	N	Y	N	Y
MD	Orders			Orders
Registered Nurse	Education			
Case Management	Facility			
Laboratory				Test
Pharmacy				Med fill
Patient	Ride		Ride	
Other		Equipment		

Now that the board is visualized, standardized, and managed in real time, the last piece to put in is accountability. This can be done by physically placing the board that is adjacent to the problem-solving board and building into the leader of morning rounds an audit of the discharge board. Discrepancies easily stand out, and any issues that senior leadership need to intervene on can be done well before the noon deadline hits.

The discharge process can now be visualized. The question becomes which discharges should be prioritized? Here, the clinical thinking that nurses are trained to use can actually hamper patient flow. Nurses are trained to provide care to the most critical patients first and then proceed down to the least critical patients. While this is excellent for patient care, it impedes the processing of discharges. Rather than focus on the most critical discharge, the focus should actually be on getting the easiest discharge out the door as quickly as possible. This will free up a bed as soon as possible so that, by the time the ED starts to get busy, there are at least one to two beds that are free on each floor.

Note that this will delay the more complex discharges to some degree. Because of that, the average time of discharge will not shift much, at least until serious problem-solving occurs. Yet, because beds are freed up sooner, flow can be improved quickly. As the hard work or truly improving the discharge process continues, the average time of discharge will slowly decrease, but do not get too focused on that metric— beds available when the ED and the PACU are ready to send patients to the floor is the real objective.

Results

The major benefit is that nursing staff, physicians, and auxiliary areas now know which discharges to focus on first. By prioritizing the easiest discharges, beds can be freed up sooner. Physicians do not need to write every order before 9 a.m., just those with a by-noon discharge that are slated. Laboratory staff now know which tests to run first to facilitate movement on the floor. While the nursing staff may not be able to do all of their discharge work in the morning, they now know what work will have the greatest impact on patient flow. By preidentifying the difficult barriers, such as the availability of a ride, gone are the days of working hard to free a bed, only to have circumstances out of the hospital's control render the effort useless.

Hospital-wide problem-solving is now possible as well. Because one of the metrics that leadership looks at every day is the number of patients who are discharged after noon for the entire hospital, and the aggregate of the causes for those defects, those areas that are consistently delaying discharges can begin problem-solving on their own boards. For instance, if case management finds that a major cause of its delays is finding skilled nursing facilities to place the patients, that raises the level of attention that is given to the issue by administration. Because they can now see the full scope of the problem, they are much better equipped to make a sound business case for pursuing new affiliations or dedicating capital to alleviate the problem.

Achieving these results takes significant time and commitment, but the rewards are significant. Simply by working the system consistently and continuously improving both its process and management, it is possible to get your arms around one of the most intractable problems in your hospital.

Chapter 10

Emergency Department

There is nothing so strong or safe in an emergency of life as the simple truth.

Charles Dickens

Introduction

Emergency departments present unique challenges due to their combination of high volume and extreme variability. Problem-solving in this environment is especially difficult because the solutions generated must work under a wide range of conditions. Patient flow issues are often multifactorial with the true causes of the issues hidden.

There are myriad problems in any ED—missing supplies, running out of meal trays, and staffing shortages or overages to name a few. The problem that a good management system excels at tackling though is patient flow through the ED.

Understanding the Problem

Patient flow is often treated as a departmental issue. For instance, the ED director is held responsible for the wait times in the ED, and the OR director is held responsible for the hold times in the PACU. In reality though, flow is interconnected, and what happens in the OR can impact flow in the ED if the floors are full.

Mapping out patient flows and looking at the wait times can identify where the blockage is. Often, this is on the floor, caused by slow discharges. Once this is addressed though, the blockage may shift to the ED.

These blockages can be thought of as kinks in an old hose. As one kink is relaxed, the next largest kink becomes the issue that limits flow. Also, as the water pressure is changed, the hose bends and flexes, alleviating some kinks while exacerbating others.

In the same way, the complexity of patient flow through the hospital means that everything is always in flux. Bottlenecks appear and disappear causing delay in the system. Traditional approaches to fixing this often run into difficulty in the ED because a system is set up around a certain patient volume and acuity and is thus thrown off when the volume and acuity change.

Developing a Solution

The answer to this problem is not to design a perfect system but rather to develop a simple method of improving the system. Applying the plan–do–study–act to the problem will start to remove the small issues that directly impact flow through the ED.

The first step is to define a fallout that can be tracked in real time. For instance, the metric may be that any patient staying in the waiting room longer than 30 minutes is considered a fallout. Each nurse can quickly track these fall-outs by simply marking a hash on an index card by the issue that caused the delay each time that they bring a patient back. At the end of the shift, the unit secretary can tally the marks and update the board. Within a few days, enough data will accumulate around the primary drivers to direct problem-solving efforts.

The driver for the delays will likely be a shortage of rooms, doctors, or nurses. This is the first *why*. At this point, the 4 wastes from Chapter 3 can be used as a guide to determine what is driving the length of time that the patient spends in the room or what tasks are pulling nurses or physicians away from patient care. The causes identified become the new Pareto chart, and data are collected until a primary driver of the first why is found. This is the second why. The cycle continues until actionable steps are identified to fix the problems.

Results

The result of this process is not only an ED that functions much more smoothly because much of the operational friction is gone, but also an ED that knows how to improve itself. Because capacity is increased due to reduced waste, the ED is more capable of withstanding the peaks of patient demand. Finally, because the staff has owned the improvement process from the beginning, the improvements made will not only stick, they will also continue to increase.

Chapter 11

Operating Rooms

The physician's highest calling, his only calling, is to make sick people healthy—to heal, as it is termed.

Samuel Hahnemann

Introduction

The OR is a complex area to manage because it is a nexus of multiple factors. The hospital measures efficiency by the room utilization rate and staff productivity, the physicians by their percentage of time in surgery, and the patients on their overall time from admissions to discharge. These competing goals invariably require trade-offs.

Layered on top of this is the variation among cases, among surgeons, and among preference cards. The supply cost in the OR is huge requiring tight management to maintain margins. Finally, the functional areas of the OR—pre-op, the ORs themselves, PACU, and sterile processing—are physically separated from each other posing a barrier to coordination. This makes managing the daily operations of the OR arguably the most difficult area of the hospital to manage.

Traditional Lean Six Sigma projects often do very well in the OR environment because so many problems revolve around the flow of supplies and patients. Thus, many of the traditional Lean tools such as value stream maps, *kanban*, and 5-S translate very nicely. Also, due to the highly regular and repeatable nature of the work, observational data are straightforward, though time consuming, to collect. Most ORs have a board runner acting as an air traffic controller. This means that someone is always watching the processes and ensuring that the various groups are coordinated and working together. This piece is missing in so many other areas of the hospital.

Board runners can be leveraged in the implementation of Lean Daily Management because they have the best visibility of what is going on. Depending upon the culture and layout of the OR, it may be advantageous to have the pre-op, OR, and PACU problem-solving boards clustered together near the board runner. This will make rounding in the OR much easier because avoiding to cross a red line can often be problematic. The downside to this approach though is that the pre-op and PACU areas may feel removed from the management process. If this is a concern, a single OR board can be initially placed and then expanded into those areas later. No matter where the board physically sits, staff from those areas should be able to easily update and present the boards daily.

Patient flow issues often become a priority in the OR. For instance, pre-op may be tracking delays that are caused by the OR, while the OR is tracking delays that are done by pre-op. When this happens, it is necessary to involve staff from both areas to solve these problems. Another issue that often arises is patient hand-off from the OR to PACU. Again, a coordinated effort to solve these problems will often be needed.

As the management system matures, it will begin to bump up against big problems, such as supply flow, equipment storage, sterile processing issues, case cart build accuracy, preference card reliability, room turnover, and so on. When this happens, this is an excellent opportunity for staff to *pull* more advanced Lean tools from the process improvement team. This is a major shift from the typical *push* approach that so often results in disengaged staff and poor sustainment of solutions.

Because the metrics on the board will be reviewed daily, this provides a high level of focus on implementing these tools. This will facilitate the process improvement team in training the staff on these tools as staff will be motivated to quickly fix the problems in order to report success. This daily rounding will also provide leadership the opportunity to hard-wire improvements.

This is most easily seen when a good 5-S project is done to organize an area that administration can walk through. Part of the 5-S process is to codify the desired state of the area visually. This makes it very easy for administration to audit the environment to ensure that the 5-S does not backslide. Note that this does not replace the manager's role in ensuring that 5-S is followed throughout the day and that the workplace is ready to begin the next day at the end of the current one.

Understanding the Problem

Because the OR lends itself naturally to competing interests and silos, *solutions* often come at the expense of other parties. The question that needs to be answered is what is the defining metric of an efficient OR? Without agreement on this, there can also be no agreement on what solutions are necessary.

Physicians can be considered customers of OR services. They, in essence, *rent* OR time (paid by the patient, of course). From a value-production perspective, the only time true value delivered to the patient is when the surgeon is operating on the patient. Therefore, it would seem that the ultimate measure of OR efficiency is the percentage of time that physicians spend in cases. As a result, the major problem to tackle seems to be the turnover time.

Yet, this may run afoul of the hospital needs to remain profitable in the OR. Hospitals must consider their labor costs in running the OR, as well as how much capital they have tied up. For them, case volume is a huge focus. This allows the fixed costs of the OR to be diluted over more cases. Also, running the OR with as few staff as possible is financially desirable. Thus, the metrics seem to be room utilization and labor hours per case. Yet, the OR turnover time has no impact on either of these metrics and may even be at odds with labor hours per case.

The key to bridging these two views is to look at the process from the perspective of the patient. There is a common misperception that Lean practitioners stress the perspective of the patient so heavily because the customer must be kept happy. While there is an element of truth to this, the real reason is that the process the customer goes through reveals where the waste is. The subtle reality is that the OR operates most efficiently when the patients do not wait in the process. In essence, this is a look at the throughput of the OR. While this seems obvious, there are a couple of counterintuitive results of this thinking.

First, while the percentage of the physician time in the OR is indeed an important metric, it is not a comprehensive metric. Instead, it is a driver of patient throughput. After all, if physicians are poorly utilized, then patients by default will languish. So, there should absolutely be an emphasis of the amount of time that physicians spend in cases versus out of them, but that is done in the larger context of patient flow.

Second, room utilization rate is a secondary metric reflecting the overall capacity of the OR as it relates to demand, not a driver of OR efficiency. (This is a bit similar to block utilization, though there are a lot of hidden problems in the block utilization metric that are outside the scope of this book.) Hospitals may define OR hours and then measure the utilization rate of rooms during those hours. If the rate is too low, they will shorten the hours to make the utilization rate artificially higher. The problem is that, while this does nothing to genuinely reduce costs, it does introduce an artificial constraint into the process—the availability of ORs.

Developing a Solution

If the unifying goal in the OR then is to keep patients moving, the next question to answer is what is the flow of the patients through the OR? This flow, as well as the flow of the supporting processes, can be mapped out to visually look at the entire process. The flow map shown in Figure 11.1 is a simplified representation of a generic OR. Note that each box can be expanded into more detailed maps of subprocesses and that different OR layouts and processes can change the map significantly. So, this map is intended to be the starting point for constructing a map that is applicable to your own hospital. More detailed maps and information can be found at LeanDailyManagement.com.

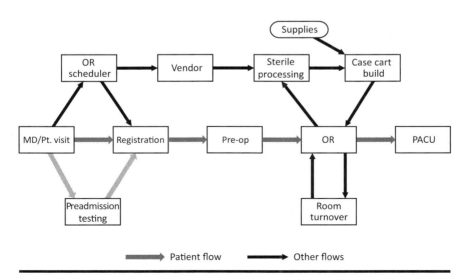

Figure 11.1   OR flow map.

This map should clearly identify the main process—patient flow—from the supporting processes. By showing the entire OR process visually, problems can be diagnosed back to their cause, supporting metrics can be created, and various OR boards can now work together cohesively to solve problems. With so many areas in the OR that could use improvement, this map will help prioritize based on the impact to patient flow. While the competing interests are not completely aligned, at least now there is open acknowledgment of those interests and a common method of balancing them.

Because this map so neatly captures the operations of the OR, and lends itself to metrics so readily, it acts as a project identifier. While the plan–do–study–act of the boards will tackle some of the issues in the OR, it will not be able to solve them all. So, the traditional Lean projects can *fit* into the map, and the boards, already aligned to the map metrics, are now queued to provide data collection and, once the project is completed, sustainment of the gains if necessary.

This map can be enhanced by dropping data onto it. Capturing the time required for each activity, as well as the average delay that occurs between them, paints a useful picture of where the flow slows down and helps identify what is blocking it. These *blockages* can be targeted with more advanced Lean initiatives to restore flow. In essence, this map becomes a diagnostic tool to ensure that the improvement team is working on the most critical area first. This helps projects improve the OR faster and helps prevent wasted effort.

Results

Now that the improvement process can be prioritized, the key is to identify key players from each functional area, including surgeons, to begin addressing issues. An experienced Lean coach is highly advised as the ORs are among the most difficult environments in which to run improvement projects.

The results of a Lean deployment in the OR can be massive. While gains achieved vary wildly based on the severity of the problems, substantial improvements should be expected. The more complex and convoluted your OR currently is, the greater the gain that can be expected, though it will take longer to achieve. For instance, throughput times for outpatients can be cut from over 8 hours to close to 5. Case cart accuracy can hit well over 90%. About 75% or better for first case on-time starts is a reasonable goal. Case studies of improvements are available at LeanDailyManagement.com for free download.

Chapter 12

Outpatient Clinics

I'm exhausted trying to stay healthy.

Steve Yzerman

Introduction

Hospitals that have outpatient clinics, often teaching hospitals, have unique challenges to running clinics efficiently without sacrificing flow in the hospital. This is because both the clinics and hospitals share the same physicians, making the integration of their schedules critical to optimizing the system. While running clinics and a hospital seems, at first glance, to complicate operations, in reality, it holds the potential to greatly simplify them. This is because hospitals that do not have their own clinics staffed by their own doctors must split the physicians' time with entities that they do not control. This can complicate things like getting timely discharge orders and scheduling block time in the OR.

Not only are physicians moving in between the clinics and hospitals but also their patients. There is often significant low-hanging fruit to facilitate better coordination of care between the hospital and the clinics. For instance, most ED visits can be seen in an urgent care clinic. If the hospital owns one that is close, significant savings can be had by implementing a medical screen-out process in the ED to route nonemergent patients to the clinic. This saves both the hospital and the patient money and helps decompress the ED to provide capacity for increased emergent volume.

Another obvious area for coordination is appointment-setting. Normally, there are a set of appointments that newborn infants need to have scheduled. Because the hospital is the first to know of the delivery, they are ideally positioned to schedule these appointments with the clinic so that the mother has preset follow-up appointments by the time that she is discharged. This same type of thinking can be used for a wide variety of patients who will need follow-up care or monitoring after they leave the inpatient units.

Even within the clinics, there is an opportunity for better coordination. Because clinics are often housed in a larger central building, there are shared resources that need to be balanced. First, parking can become an issue because parking codes are based on the assumption of the average number of visits per day, broken down to an average hourly number. If clinic volumes fluctuate significantly throughout the day, this can become an issue. Central registration is sometimes used as well. This can become a bottleneck to flowing patients into the rooms to see their provider.

If there is no one at all of the clinics as a system, then efforts to locally optimize each clinic will exacerbate these problems. Providers typically like to frontload the schedule so that there is always a patient who is ready to be seen. This makes the provider's day very efficient. The problem though is that, any time that there is a delay, the default response is to frontload the schedule more. This results in the system bottleneck, such as parking and central registration, getting worse as the patient volume spikes early in the morning, and drops sharply for the rest of the day.

Understanding the Problem

These problems stem from the natural inclination for clinics to be isolated. Because their view of patient flow begins and ends at the clinic door, the links with other clinics, the ED, and the hospital inpatient units are lost. These links though are not lost on the patients who are frustrated by their inability to schedule appointments in multiple clinics easily. They are frustrated by the difficulties in registration, the long wait times, and the effort that is required to simply get into the room to see the provider. From the patients' perspective, all of the clinics, the ED, the OR, and the floors are all part of the same hospital, so why do they all function independently? Bringing this perspective into clinics can go a long way to broadening the view of the staff and physicians and help fix the holes in management.

One of the challenges facing the person overseeing all of the clinics is the inability to see the work that occurs in each of them. For instance, how can he or she manage overall patient flow and decrease wait times when the schedules are owned and visible only to the individual clinics? Like so many of the other problems in the hospital, the difficulty in seeing what is happening when curtails the ability of management to address and solve issues. Small things that are difficult to spot, such as provider tardiness, can create large problems elsewhere that are difficult to diagnose, and, without proper diagnoses, treatment plans are impossible to accurately craft.

Developing a Solution

Despite the complexity of the problems, or more precisely, because of that complexity, the approach to fixing them must be simple. As you have seen in the rest of the book, the simple, consistent application of the plan–do–study–act cycle to detect symptoms, diagnose problems, and then treat the problems will slowly and steadily root out entrenched problems and gradually calm the chaos. The clinics are no different in principle but, in practice, will need some tweaking.

The first problem is to figure out where to start deploying Lean Daily Management. This will be an issue because there are a lot of clinics, each with their own culture and problems. As in the hospital, you should start wherever is easiest to implement. By using the *Law of Interconnected Waste*, we know that system problems will be uncovered no matter where we dig; thus, it only makes sense to dig where the soil is softest.

Like the rest of the hospital, the clinics will need to go through their own cultural progression, and, like the hospital, they will go through the same phases and can be tracked using the same audit tool. One thing that leaders should be ready for though is that, because clinic staff have worked in isolation for years, bringing them into the fold and treating them as part of the hospital team focused on patient flow will yield both great enthusiasm and, in some cases, strong resistance. Overall, expect them to reach integration faster than hospital units. Because of this, clinics should be the last area that is brought up on the management system.

The next thing to consider is the span of control and the reporting structure. Usually, clinic managers report to a central clinic director or the vice-president. Yet, patients flow from the clinics to the hospital and back again, jumping this span of control. When daily rounds are set up in the clinics, the central clinic director should be the one to own them. This allows the director to see every clinic every day and get a good feel for the challenges facing the clinics as a whole. Also, because the managers report to the director either directly or through an additional layer of management, it allows a daily conversation between the central clinic director and the managers.

As the clinics become ready to become more integrated in their problem-solving with the hospital, key hospital leaders should attend clinic rounds at least once a week. For instance, the head of women and children should walk the boards in the women's and children's clinics, the OR director should walk the boards in the surgical clinics, the ED director should walk the boards in the urgent care clinics, and so on. This allows these leaders to look at the wider patient flow and coordinate clinic/hospital problem-solving. This will help prevent local fixes that would create a backlog in the ED, such as the urgent care clinic closing early.

This rounding by hospital leaders in the clinics will also help them see the physicians' perspective because they are now looking at the entire work cycle of the provider. As any doctor will attest, not every hospital improvement initiative makes life easier for them. Because they are such an integral part of the hospital—in essence, the hospital exists to facilitate contact between the doctor and the patient— understanding the structure of their day and the challenges they face is every bit as important as looking through the nurses' eyes.

This is another reason to hold the clinics last in the rollout. Because leadership has such a steep learning curve, it is best that physicians are not involved until later. As leaders become comfortable and confident with the new management system, they will be prepared to sell the concept to the physicians, withstand the initial, inevitable criticism, and use the system to solve problems that are important to the doctors.

Some good clinic-specific metrics to use are as follows:

- *Number of late appointments*—This can be broken down by late provider, provider with other patients, support staff unavailable, no parking, patient late, registration late, etc.
- *Number of patients waiting longer than 10 minutes for registration*—This can be broken down by cause (registration staff unavailable, patient early, etc.), patient type (orthopedic, obstetrics and gynecology, pediatrics,

etc.), or time of day (i.e., 8–10 a.m., 10 a.m.–12 noon, 12 noon–2 p.m., or 2–4 p.m.).

■ *Number of overbooked appointments*—In an effort to fill time slots, clinics will often overbook. This metric can help dig into why these overbookings are happening.

■ *Number of patient no-shows*—There is usually a high no-show rate in clinics, especially pediatric clinics. Digging in to this and finding out why each patient did not show can help reduce the occurrence.

Results

Once the clinics are up and running and the staff have progressed through the cultural continuum, the first result is that they will be much more tightly integrated with the hospital and actively driving toward a common strategic goal. For instance, one of the strategic goals will be to increase the volumes of certain types of patients. The clinics impacted by this goal will see where they currently are, and where they need to be, and identify problems that need to be addressed to close the gap. Increased surgical volumes may drive patient volumes to unsustainable levels in the clinics, requiring expansion of the clinic area or a reduction in the goal. By identifying these constraints early, the leadership team can make decisions proactively to avoid strategic implementation failures.

The second result will be a more engaged staff. Because clinic staff are physically removed from the hospital, they often feel isolated and uninformed on the happenings at the hospital. By involving hospital leaders in rounds, and by involving clinic staff in addressing hospital problems, this perception can be reduced.

The third major result will be a better understanding of physicians and the barriers that they encounter in delivering care. This gives the hospital the opportunity to proactively and holistically care for their doctors. Given that most medical staffs are not contractually bound to a particular hospital, this is a competitive advantage that can be used.

The fourth and final result is that opportunities to deliver a greater continuity of care will be found. As patient service increases, it will naturally become hardwired by the staff who fix the problems, making it incredibly difficult for competitors to replicate.

Chapter 13

Quality

*I would rather discover one true cause than gain the
kingdom of Persia.*

Democritus

Introduction

Clinical quality improvement continues to be a vexing problem
for hospitals. As reimbursement becomes increasingly depen-
dent upon quality outcomes, this not only presents a serious patient safety issue for hospitals but also a financial one.
Historically, process improvement departments, be they based
on Lean, Six Sigma, or some other approach, have existed
independently of quality departments. This is unfortunate
because process improvement hinges on quality improvement,
and quality cannot improve without improved processes. The
two are intractably linked.

There is often tension between the hospital and the quality
department when a Lean Daily Management system is rolled
out. This tension is both understandable and unnecessary.
Because the boards do not *belong* to the Lean department or

the Lean champion but rather the units on which they reside, there is absolutely nothing preventing them from attacking quality problems. Because quality departments often have their own quality improvement boards on the units, there is a natural turf battle that can break out. Therefore, it is highly advisable to bring the quality people into the fold as early as possible.

That said, there are significant risks to bringing them in too soon, and, because these risks vary greatly by hospital, it will be up to you and your Lean coach to determine when is the right time. The following discussion is then intended to help you make that decision.

When evaluating the timing of integrating quality with the boards, the first thing to consider is the history of the relationship between the quality department and nursing. Many quality departments have a tendency to treat all quality problems as compliance problems. This can be seen in the recommended steps to prevent future errors. Often, there is a human resources component to them, such as making offenses punishable by mandatory suspension, written warnings, and so on. As covered earlier in Chapter 5, not only does that approach to fixing problems not work; it also severely undermines the legitimacy of the daily management system that you are trying to build.

The danger is if the quality department is given too much control before they themselves have undergone a culture change that the boards will become daily whipping posts that are used to excoriate yesterday's offenses. Because this will kill trust, possibly permanently, it must be avoided at all costs. Be aware of the culture and tone that currently exists in the quality department when bringing them in to avoid this problem.

Another major challenge when integrating your quality people is that they usually have a different approach to problem-solving. It is common for them to be very heavy on the data collection and analysis, usually in a monthly cadence, and to focus on generating reports. Yet, when it comes to actually implementing fixes, they struggle. The reason for this is that their data, while exhaustive, are historical. They can say *what* happened with great accuracy, yet they struggle to answer *why* it happened. As such, they are forced to rely on best guesses and intuition. This is very similar to the current state of most hospital administrations.

The trick will be to help them to understand the value of real-time data and plan–do–study–act (PDSA) problem-solving. This is a major leap for them because so much effort has been on generating data of the highest quality possible (despite the delay that it causes) that to shift toward real-time, incomplete data is difficult. Once they understand the power behind the PDSA method though, the quality people will become some of the biggest champions for the boards.

Once you are ready to start integrating quality, the next question is to figure out where and how to do so. You would want to focus on a floor, preferably nursing, that is bumping up against a quality problem yet also has a mature-enough culture to be able to withstand a few missteps from the quality department as they learn the process. The quality people will make mistakes and push the process too hard at first. That is actually a good thing. You will need to find a floor though that will not become defensive to that.

Once you have identified a floor and they have identified the quality metric that they want to focus on, the next step is to identify the quality person who is responsible for that metric. At your hospital, this may just be the person who is responsible for reporting that metric.

There are a lot of ways to bring the team together. One way is to help the unit turn the quality metric into a fallout and start tracking it on their board. Let that run for a week or so, and then invite the quality person on that round. Most of the time, this will stimulate good discussion at the board. The key here is that the unit has a head start and already has data by the time the quality department has their first look at the metric. This satisfies the analytical side of the quality person and brings him or her in close to the point where the unit is ready to start trying some problem-solving. It is a very natural entry point for an outside expert, the quality person, and subtly puts him or her in the position of being coached by the unit.

As the problem begins to get solved, the quality department will start to see the value of the system and will want to see more quality metrics in more areas of the hospital. Be aware that this point is coming and that you will likely need to put some pressure on the brakes at that point. Force them to prioritize and focus on just one quality metric per area. Then, take that to only the floors that are ready, and give it to them as an option for them to work on. If they are not yet ready, do not force it—at some point in the near future, they will run out of easy things to work on and will circle back to the quality need.

When the system is mature, the quality department will no longer be pushing and owning quality. They will continue to monitor quality and identify weak spots, but their role will become that of an expert resource who are called in to the units when they get stuck on a metric or do not know how to attack a problem. The units will possess their own quality, and they will pull on the quality department as needed to achieve their quality goals.

Then, with this larger overview in mind, let us look at how this system can improve specific quality metrics throughout the hospital.

Understanding the Problem

Because problem-solving on the board happens daily, the best problems to address are the ones that occur with enough frequency to generate enough data to dig into the root cause. Many quality metrics, such as surgical site infection, happen too infrequently, and, by the time they happen, the cause is difficult to determine. They are not good board metrics. However, the boards can still be used to improve these measures if the drivers for these problems can be identified and tracked.

For instance, one metric often used by intensive care units is the number of times that people enter the unit without washing their hands. Because this is a known risk factor, this problem, which happens multiple times a day, can be improved under the theory that hospital-acquired infections, which happen infrequently, will improve as well. This is where the experience of the quality nurse is critical. Because the first layer of causes is based on quality theory rather than process-generated data, a solid quality professional is needed to guide the team to the most likely drivers of the quality fall-out to start their PDSA problem-solving.

Most quality metrics will fall into this category. The more complex ones can be broken down into their drivers. Falls, for instance, have well-documented best practices for their prevention. The trick though is to determine which driver to focus on. This is a departure from the standard way of improving quality. Normally, a host of fall prevention measures are checked monthly to ensure compliance. This is not necessarily bad, but it is difficult to problem-solve multiple factors at a time. Thus, the role of the quality nurse is to determine which factor is the most critical for problem-solving. This will become the quality metric for the board.

There are two basic approaches that can be used: (1) unit-centric and (2) hospital-wide. The unit-centric approach is faster and easier than the hospital-wide approach and should be the starting point for infusing quality into the boards. With this approach, quality data by floor need to be analyzed, and the primary quality fallout along with its primary driver is identified. This driver then becomes the unit metric for them to work. As that driver is solved, the impact on the quality metric can be monitored (if the failure rate is high

enough), and the staff can move on to the next most promi-
nent driver.

This approach will feel slow, but, like every other aspect
of implementing a management system, go slow to go fast.
Because the staff is focused on one specific problem, it is
much easier to diagnose the problem and hardwire a treatment plan. Also, initially, focusing on issues floor by floor
will build the problem-solving skills that are needed to merge
quality metrics with the board.

As the hospital develops, a broader approach to quality will
become possible. The units will be able to handle much of the
problem-solving on their own with assistance as needed from
the quality staff. Using this approach, hospital-wide quality
metrics can be addressed in an organized manner with data
flowing from the unit-level boards to the administration board.
For instance, if falls are the focus of the hospital, a common
metric, such as not identifying a fall-risk patient, or falsely
identifying a patient who is not a fall risk, can be aggregated
to look at the problem systematically. This can lead to hospital-
level root-cause analysis to look at hospital-level ways to fix the
problem.

Developing a Solution

As the drivers to quality problems are identified, actions can
be taken to correct them. This can happen at a unit or hospital level, depending on the scope. These solutions may
or may not work. By testing them though in the context of
Lean Daily Management, we can eliminate the bad solutions
quickly. Because data are gathered daily instead of monthly,
management of the quality improvement process can be done
continuously.

Because Lean Daily Management has a bias toward action,
the way that data are collected and reported will necessarily change. Quality departments tend to be reporting-centric

with a heavy emphasis on accurate and complete data. While this is valuable, it is also slow. Daily management instead values usefulness and immediacy over accuracy and completeness. So, for instance, while working to improve fall preventions, quality departments may dig deep to establish how many patients were not diagnosed as a fall risk, whereas Lean Daily Management will seek to understand the primary driver behind missed diagnoses. This will feel like a way of cutting corners to the quality staff and so is not a good replacement for the reporting system that they currently have in place. It is there to augment the information that is available to put the emphasis back on root-cause analysis and problem-solving. As the quality team becomes more comfortable with Lean Daily Management, they will likely streamline their own reporting standards to better align with the needs of the boards.

Results

The ultimate goal of infusing quality into the daily management system is more than to simply solve quality problems; the goal is also to proactively manage the drivers of quality daily so that quality is built into the care process. In essence, by making the drivers of quality visible on a daily basis, small corrections can be made to the process before the patients or the quality metrics are adversely affected.

This is similar to the thinking behind using a failure modes and effects analysis (FMEA) to manage quality, except that it is arrived at methodically and managed continuously. FMEAs essentially ask all the possible drivers of adverse outcomes to be thought of and ranked by the likelihood of occurrence and potential impact. The problem is that of the unknown unknowns. Preemptive root-cause analysis is impossible in a complex environment because there are no real, tangible data to link drivers to outcomes. Instead, there is speculation and hypothesis rather than observation and data. Infusing quality into the daily management system bridges this gap.

If your hospital is already using FMEAs, they can be validated and managed with the management system. First, the drivers of fallouts can be observed. Their frequency and impact can be objectively measured. This results in an FMEA with properly weighted drivers.

The next piece though is that these drivers can be managed daily by management and accountability that are enforced by leadership. The Lean Daily Management system morphs into a daily quality management system. This system can monitor quality at both the unit and hospital level and provide leadership with early detection of lapses in quality, often before harm occurs.

Chapter 14

Patient Satisfaction

Beware the fury of a patient man.

John Dryden

Introduction

Healthcare is unique in the sense that the work is done on the customers rather than simply for the customers. Yet, while the customers have very little understanding of the intricacies of the work that is done, they are still expected to make major decisions about the next steps that have severe implications on their quality of life. Given the combination of pain and invasive procedures, clinical ignorance, and high-pressured decisions, the last outcome to be expected should be patient satisfaction, yet that is precisely a metric that hospital payments hinge upon.

All is not lost, however. The secret, like the solution to most operational problems, lies with the care providers—nurses and physicians. Poor treatment of patients rightfully enrages those who have dedicated their lives to their service.

Understanding the Problem

Poor data plague efforts to improve the patient experience. They are compiled monthly, usually by a third party, and averaged together. This delay and loss of detail make finding the cause of problems difficult. Worse yet, for problem-solving, the hospital averages are then compared against many other hospitals, and, rather than an average, a percentile is reported. The resulting number bears little resemblance to the actual performance of the hospital, yet that metric is used to determine reimbursement and bonuses. Great celebrations are held when a few tenths of a point of improvement are made in one month, and heads roll when a few tenths of a percent are lost by the next month. Yet, small sample sizes, natural variation, and comparison against other hospitals as opposed to self-comparison all combine to make these month-to-month variations meaningless.

The two core problems are that the data are reported by fallouts, making measuring progress difficult, and the data are historical, making root-cause problem-solving near impossible. The solution then is to accurately capture fallouts and do so as they occur. In short, this can be tackled with your daily management system.

Developing a Solution

Typical HCAHPS data are useful for identifying the starting point for improving patient satisfaction. A thorough analysis of the data and careful reading of patient comments will highlight the weak areas where the hospital needs to focus. Like everything else, with Lean Daily Management, the idea is to look for the outliers. What specific floor or supporting unit is the primary driver of the problem? While it is tempting to force an HCAHPS metric on every board, the opposite should

028 55 09

322 8042 →

$130 \div 500$
$+130$
$500 = 630$

PREFERRED

866-965-4560

Kontinuous

☆ read **10 pages** of psychology
★ read 10 pages of Qoran
☆ Read 10 pages of Masnavi
☆ read Apply for jobs (2 hrs)

be done—focus on as few areas as possible to achieve gains as quickly as possible.

A good starting metric is the *number of patient complaints.* This will need to be gathered daily, which means that some sort of auditing system will need to be developed. This can be as simple as customer comment cards or a staff member visiting a certain number of patients each day at random to gather their input. While this sampling method is fraught with bias, it will not impede the problem-solving process. Timely, useful data beat delayed, accurate data. The magic is in the Pareto chart, not the run chart, so, as long as the driver of the complaint is captured, the process will work.

Results

As the plan–do–study–act process works through the problem, other areas may be brought in to support. For instance, low scores on nursing floors often can be traced back to EVS or dietary. When this happens, be careful not to let the floor *fix* their problem at the expense of another floor. This can happen if the EVS manager, for instance, knows that administration is watching a particular floor carefully. They will shift resources to that area starving the other floors. Usually, problems like these will need to be resolved by increasing support staff or streamlining the support processes. Either way, your team now has hard data to guide that decision.

Chapter 15

Conclusion

*Knowledge gained through experience is far superior
and many times more useful than bookish knowledge.*

Mahatma Gandhi

You now have a complete picture of how a Lean Daily
Management system works. You know the steps to implement
on in your organization. You can see how such a system can
impact the large, deeply rooted problems that exist in your
hospital. Yet, true learning is in the doing and teaching, not
the reading.

No book, no course, and no amount of studying can fully
prepare you for the intricacies of redesigning how your hospital's operations are managed. The best that can be achieved is
to understand the broad strokes of the path and the ultimate
destination. As is so often the case, you will not know what
you need to know until you have learned it.

So, then, your first step is to take your first step. Put
together a route plan. Huddle with your fellow leaders to
establish True North and a basic set of hospital metrics. Push
training out to your staff and managers. (Free training material can be found at LeanDailyManagement.com/downloads.)
Design boards, and let your staff choose where to hang them.

If you decide to bring in outside expertise, start setting up interviews and gathering quotes.

As you start your Lean journey, never forget that the journey is not about doing but rather about becoming. The secret to success in implementing a Lean management system is consistency and self-discipline on the part of leadership. All other mistakes and failures are recoverable. When in doubt, go slow. Let the data lead the way. Drop preconceptions about what can and cannot be addressed. When all else fails, trust your staff—no one knows their work better than they do.

Glossary

CMS: Centers for Medicare & Medicaid Services.

CVU: Cardiovascular unit.

D/C: Discharge.

ED: Emergency department.

EHR: Electronic health record.

EMR: Electronic medical record.

EVS: Environmental services.

HCAHPS: Hospital Consumer Assessment of Healthcare Providers and Systems. HCAPHS scores are patient satisfaction scores that are used to rank hospitals.

HIPAA: The Health Insurance Portability and Accountability Act of 1996 patient confidentiality law.

HMO: Health maintenance organization.

ICU: Intensive care unit.

L&D: Labor and delivery.

LVN: Licensed vocational nurse. This is a nurse with a lower level of training than an RN and, while cheaper, is limited in scope.

MD: Doctor, physician.

MHA: Masters of healthcare administration.

MICU: Medicine intensive care unit.

NICU: Neurointensive care unit *or* neonatal intensive care unit.

OR: Operating room. This can refer to a specific operating room or the entire department, including the pre-op area and the PACU.

PACU: Postanesthesia care unit. This is the where surgery patients recover.

PICU: Pediatric intensive care unit.

Pre-op: Preoperative area. This is where patients are prepped for surgery.

PT: Physical therapy.

Pt.: Patient.

RN: Registered nurse.

SICU: Surgical intensive care unit.

STAT: Short for *statim*, Latin for "immediately."

TAT: Turnaround time.

Index

This index includes the front matter. Page numbers in front matter are in italics; f, n, and t refer to figures, footnotes, and tables, respectively.